THE CHINESE PEOPLE'S MOVEMENT

PERSPECTIVES ON SPRING 1989

THE CHINESE PEOPLE'S MOVEMENT

PERSPECTIVES ON SPRING 1989

EDITED BY
TONY SAICH

AN EAST GATE BOOK

M. E. SHARPE, INC.
ARMONK, NEW YORK/LONDON, ENGLAND

An East Gate Book

Copyright © 1990 by M. E. Sharpe, Inc.

Available in the United Kingdom and Europe from M. E. Sharpe, Publishers,
3 Henrietta Street, London WC2E 8LU.

Library of Congress Cataloging-in-Publication Data

The Chinese people's movement : perspectives on spring 1989 / edited by
   Tony Saich.
    p. cm.
   Includes index.
   ISBN 0-87332-745-4   ISBN 0-87332-746-2 (pbk.)
   1. China—History—Tiananmen Square Incident, 1989. I. Saich, Tony.
DS779.32.C5   1990
951.05′8—dc20   90-41535
                                                                         CIP

Printed in the United States of America.

MV 10 9 8 7 6 5 4 3 2 1

CONTENTS

THE PRODEMOCRACY demonstrations of April–May and their brutal suppression in June 1989 have left a major impression on all who witnessed them. The age of satellite television meant that the events were beamed into homes throughout the world. The demonstrations revealed an urban population that was frustrated with the half-baked reforms that were on offer. In a dramatic way, they represented the emergence of public opinion in urban China. The bloody suppression revealed a Communist Party leadership that was severely out of touch with its own society and the consequences of its own desire for economic progress. In calling on the army to suppress the movement, the leadership revealed how shallow the political reforms had been to date. It made a mockery of its own claims that a system of "rule by (party) man" had been replaced by one of "rule by law."

Beijing's current leaders have shown no remorse for their actions. Indeed, whenever offered an opportunity, they have persisted in asserting that the actions were fully justified, and that, rather than being condemned, they should be congratulated for their tough response. The dramatic events in Eastern Europe that unfolded during the latter part of 1989 have further convinced the leadership that it was right to crack down hard on the protesters. They have retreated into the "safety" of the shell provided by central planning and have threatened society with further violence unless it comes to heel.

The bloodshed in Beijing was interpreted differently, however, by some Communist parties in Eastern Europe. It acted as a spur to dialogue with the emerging civil society; the only alternative was to repeat the bloody scenes of Beijing. Fortunately, in East Germany and Czechoslovakia there were sufficiently enlightened leaders to recognize this fact. The violent attempts to suppress the demonstrations in Rumania showed, however, that China did not stand entirely alone in its advocacy of force for solving societal problems. The subsequent fall of Ceausescu must have come as a shock for Beijing's leaders and encouraged those who had challenged authoritarian party rule.

Despite the outward appearance of strength, the Chinese leadership has been revealed as weak, internally divided, and out of step with the forces of change that are sweeping much of the Communist world. While the leaders may be able to maintain power over the short term, they cannot rule continuously without the support of key sectors of their urban society. The current policy prescription can be summed up as "back to the future." The political dinosaurs who rule China dream of a bygone "golden age" when there was social stability and solid economic growth under an essentially Soviet-style economic system, and when it was clear who were enemies and who were friends.

Such an approach has nothing to offer to a modernizing China that has to function in an increasingly complex world. Eventually, China will have to return to the path of reform; the question remains when and under what circumstances. Populations do not take kindly to leaders who are willing to set loose tanks on them. Unless reformers can take power from within the party, the party, having lost any residual legitimacy, faces being swept away by a further round of social unrest.

Over the long term, we are most likely to be dealing with a reform-minded party leadership or possibly a China no longer ruled by the Communist Party. Policy makers would be well advised to bear this in mind when dwelling on short-term strategic issues. One thing is quite clear: the West does not need China. The strategic reasons that underpinned previous policy have been eroded by the dramatic changes in both the Soviet Union and Eastern Europe. Business has more than enough opportunities to exploit in these evolving markets. Indeed, even before the events of 1989, foreign business was becoming more realistic about the realities of the China market. Now, it should be even more cautious about rushing to invest in an unstable environment. Thus, if we want to continue dealings with China, it should be on our terms rather than on those set by a harsh, authoritarian regime.

The idea for this book developed among a group of us working in the Netherlands. It took a more definite shape during a conference held at Brandeis University entitled ''Perspectives on Tiananmen 1989'' held in mid-September 1989. In discussions in and around the conference, the American contributors agreed to participate. It was decided that each author would determine for herself or himself exactly how the movement would be referred to. Thus, there was no attempt to produce a uniform terminology.

While this book tries to set the movement in a broader perspective, it is not the intention to impose an order or rationality that did not exist. Much of what happened on Tiananmen Square was spontaneous and the result of circumstance. Many of those who participated did so for vague reasons. Beyond the idea that things were wrong and should change, many had no concrete proposals for ideas of change. Once started, the movement gained its own momentum, and some joined in simply because it was fun to humiliate a bunch of old men locked up in their governmental fortresses. Rather then detracting from the integrity of the movement, this makes the authority's resort to massive violence all the more pathetic.

I would like to thank Tim Cheek, who got us in touch with Doug Merwin of M. E. Sharpe. Both showed enthusiasm at a crucial stage. My thanks go to all those involved, and especially to those Chinese friends who have helped me over the years in my dealings with the People's Republic. I can only say that I hope you may live to see more peaceful times.

Tony Saich
Amsterdam, December 1989

CONTRIBUTORS

Woei Lien Chong is a researcher at the Documentation and Research Centre for Contemporary China, Sinological Institute, Leiden University, and coeditor of the quarterly journal *China Information*.

Seth Faison is a reporter with the Beijing Bureau of the *South China Morning Post*.

Kathleen Hartford is an associate professor of Political Science at the University of Massachusetts in Boston and a researcher at Harvard's Fairbank Center for East Asian Research.

Nancy Hearst is a librarian at Harvard's Fairbank Center for East Asian Research.

Stefan R. Landsberger is a researcher at the Documentation and Research Centre for Contemporary China, Sinological Institute, Leiden University, and coeditor of the quarterly journal *China Information*.

Frank Niming conducted anthropological fieldwork in Beijing from late 1988 until June 1989.

Tony Saich is a professor at the Sinological Institute, Leiden University, and a senior research fellow at the International Institute of Social History, Amsterdam.

Lawrence R. Sullivan is an associate professor in the Department of Political Science, Adelphi University, Garden City, New York, and a research associate at the East Asian Institute, Columbia University.

Jeffrey N. Wasserstrom is an assistant professor in the Department of History, University of Kentucky.

ABBREVIATIONS

BSAF	Beijing Students' Autonomous Federation
BWAF	Beijing Workers' Autonomous Federation
CAD	China Alliance for Democracy
CCP	Chinese Communist Party
FDC	Front for a Democratic China
NPC	National People's Congress

THE CHINESE PEOPLE'S MOVEMENT

PERSPECTIVES ON
SPRING 1989

One

STUDENT PROTESTS AND THE CHINESE TRADITION, 1919–1989

Jeffrey N. Wasserstrom

THE MOMENTOUS events of the spring of 1989 were in many regards unprecedented in the annals of Chinese history. Never before had the international news media focused such intense scrutiny upon a Chinese youth movement, presenting television viewers around the world with pictures of student banners within days or even minutes of the time these flags first appeared on the streets. Never before had group hunger fasts figured so prominently in a Chinese student movement. Never before had youths in Beijing and Shanghai rallied around statues of the "Goddess of Democracy." And never before in the history of the nation's student movements had Chinese troops killed so many unarmed students and sympathizers in so short a time, as they did in and around Tiananmen Square during the massacre of June 3 and 4.

This piece evolved out of my attempt to write an epilogue for the manuscript version of my doctoral thesis. Documentation to support the claims about pre-1949 student movements I make in the following pages can be found in my dissertation, "Taking It to the Streets: Shanghai Students and Political Protests, 1919–1949" (University of California at Berkeley, 1989). Earlier versions of this chapter were presented at the New England China Seminar at Harvard University and at an East Asian colloquium at Indiana University. I am grateful to those who attended these two talks for their helpful suggestions and criticisms. I would also like to thank Anne Bock, Janice Kelly, and Sebastian Heilmann for reading and commenting upon earlier drafts of this chapter.

Novelties such as these aside, however, the Democracy Uprising of 1989 was in many ways strikingly reminiscent of the great student-led popular struggles of China's Republican era (1911–1949), such as the May Fourth Movement of 1919 and the December Ninth Movement of 1935. There was nothing novel, for example, about the fact that the largest mass actions of 1989 ended up paralyzing major Chinese cities, since general strikes in which student protesters played pivotal roles had brought the bustling commercial hub of Shanghai to a standstill for days at a time during both 1919 and 1925. There was also nothing new about many of the issues that motivated participants in the Democracy Uprising to take action, since complaints about official corruption and censorship had helped trigger student protests throughout the first half of the twentieth century. And there was nothing novel about the way in which the Democracy Uprising led foreign observers to speculate about whether the CCP was losing or had lost its mandate to rule, since the student-led anti-hunger, anti–Civil War Movement of 1947 made many Westerners ask the same questions about the then dominant Nationalist Party.

In addition, when it came to publicizing their grievances, the participants turned to many of the same propaganda techniques their predecessors of the Republican era had used. When a leader of the Democracy Uprising bit her finger to write out a poster criticizing Li Peng in her own blood, for example, she was replicating an act student protesters had performed in 1915 and 1919. The students of 1989 were also not the first to send lecture brigades to factories to court worker support, organize teams of bicyclists to spread word of government actions from one part of the city to another, and hang bloodstained clothes of the martyrs from campus gates to publicize official brutality—educated youths had done all of these things in 1925 during the May Thirtieth Movement. And when participants in the Democracy Uprising chanted "People's Army don't harm the people," this too was an act with clear historical precedents, since in the mid-

1940s student protesters had often shouted "Chinese people shouldn't beat up Chinese people" (*Zhongguoren buda Zhongguoren*) at the police who came to break up demonstrations and rallies. Sometimes the students of 1989 even put new words to the exact same tunes their predecessors of the Republican era had sung. To cite but one particularly bizarre example, in both 1947 and 1989 Chinese students put new lyrics to Frère Jacques, turning the French air into a song of protest.

The similarities between past and present were also strong where protest tactics, slogans, and organizational strategies were concerned. When the students of 1989 staged classroom strikes, swore collective oaths to persevere until death to carry out their mission, paraded under banners emblazoned with the names of their schools, rallied to the cry of "Long Live Democracy" (*minzhu wansui*), and claimed that they had a special role and duty as intellectuals to lead the nation's citizens in a fight to "save the nation" (*jiuguo*)—in each of these instances the youthful participants in the Democracy Uprising replicated the actions and echoed the cries of their predecessors of the Republican era. When the youths occupying Tiananmen Square formed a complex bureaucratic structure, complete with a student police force to maintain order and special departments with assigned heads to take care of things such as finances and relations with the foreign press, this was also far from unprecedented. Participants in the May Fourth Movement and other student-led struggles of the Republican era had established similar shadow governments to keep order within their movements.

The Rebirth of the May Fourth Tradition

The existence of continuities such as those noted above provides reason enough to look back to events of China's pre-Communist past when trying to make sense of the heroism and tragedy of 1989. But there is another, equally compelling reason to do so: the students themselves viewed their actions as part of a time-honored historical tradition of patriotic political engagement. This is not to say that all of the parallels between past and present that emerged in 1989 were intentional. In some cases, when participants in the Democracy Uprising resurrected tactics and symbols associated with protests of the Republican era, they were doubtless completely unaware of the historical precedents involved. In other cases, however, the students of 1989 were clearly quite conscious of the connections between past and present; at times these youths took great pains to present their struggle as a continuation of earlier battles against oppression.

This awareness of the past manifested itself in varying ways. It showed through in the slogans student protesters chose for their banners, since some youths carried flags referring to "Mr. Science" and "Mr. Democracy," terms intimately associated with the May Fourth Movement of 1919. It also showed through in student wall posters, some of which were filled with allusions to the December Ninth Movement of 1935 and other Republican era struggles. Had Hu Yaobang (the former general secretary of the CCP, who had been dismissed from office two years before for his lenient handling of an earlier wave of prodemocracy protests) lived a month longer, the historical consciousness of the students might have determined the exact timing of the Democracy Uprising's birth. Long before Hu's death, student activists in Beijing and other cities had been planning to use the occasion of the seventieth anniversary of the May Fourth Movement to start a new round of demonstrations protesting governmental corruption and the slow pace of political reform. Thus, when Hu succumbed to a heart attack on April 15, this merely meant that the students had a reason to take to the streets two weeks ahead of schedule.

Despite this rearrangement of the precise timetable of revolt, historical precedents still ended up playing a crucial role in shaping the earliest phase of the Democracy Uprising. To begin with, when the students staged demonstrations that simultaneously honored Hu's memory and raised criticisms of contemporary authorities, they were following in a well-established tradition of using funerary rites to express a renewed commitment to political change. Throughout the twentieth century, China's educated youths have consistently marked in this fashion the deaths of martyrs and prominent figures associated with the cause of reform, and mass memorial marches have frequently played a key role in either triggering or escalating the development of student movements. Prior to 1989 this had happened most recently in April 1976, when enormous crowds of students and other citizens had descended upon Tiananmen Square to mourn Zhou Enlai and criticize the "Gang of Four." The history of the Republican era is filled with similar cases, beginning with the protests professors and students staged after the revolutionary political leader Song Jiaoren was assassinated in 1913. More often than not, however, the martyrs students mourned during the Republican era were not famous figures at all, but rather classmates and workers who died while taking part in patriotic marches. Memorial services cum protests for martyrs of this sort played central roles in the growth of the popular movements of 1919, 1925, 1945, and other years.

If the echoes of the past were strong during the late-April demonstrations honoring Hu Yaobang, however, they became a roar when the May Fourth anniversary finally arrived. Though the demonstrations held on this date did not inaugurate the Democracy Uprising, they served as one of the key turning points in the growth of the movement. When educated youths defied government directives to refrain from protesting and came together in the same square where their predecessors of seventy years before had gathered, this was a tremendously important symbolic act, especially since the student demonstration successfully upstaged the festivities CCP officials themselves put on to mark the revolutionary anniversary date. The student protest of May 4 showed that the participants in the Democracy Uprising were determined to make their movement more than just another short-lived series of protests, of the sort that had taken place from December of 1986 through early January 1987. It also gave the government its first real indication that the popular movement might pose a threat not only to political order but to the very political legitimacy of the CCP as well.

The Legacy of 1919

Why was this particular march so important? To answer this, one must begin by understanding what took place in 1919, and the special symbolic role the May Fourth anniversary has come to play in the Chinese political calendar. The May Fourth Movement was named after the date when police in Beijing arrested and beat up scores of student marchers for taking part in a demonstration protesting certain terms of the Treaty of Versailles, under which the World War I allies would transfer control of parts of China formerly under German rule to Japan, rather than returning the territories to the Chinese. The youths who took to the streets that day, though primarily concerned with the international dispute, were also intensely critical of their country's own government, a corrupt and repressive warlord regime that seemed all too willing to appease Japanese imperialists even if it meant sacrificing China's national sovereignty. Soon, like so many student movements in so many times and places, the May Fourth Movement became as much a fight for the right to protest as a struggle against imperialism and corruption.

During the weeks that followed the first arrests of student protesters, the May Fourth Movement grew into a struggle that surpassed all previous Chinese youth movements in terms of size and scope. Inspired by the bravery of the original Beijing protesters, and angered by the way the authorities had tried to suppress nonviolent protests by the flower of the nation's youth, urban Chinese of all classes joined in the patriotic movement. The students remained at the center of the struggle, as educated youths in various cities staged sympathy demonstrations and classroom strikes; organized lecture teams to spread word of the events of the "May Fourth Tragedy" and the terms of the Treaty of Versailles to the masses; drafted petitions of protest to send to governmental authorities; and formed the first citywide and then national student associations to coordinate protest activities. Merchants, workers, and members of virtually all other urban social groups (ranging from prostitutes and pickpockets to schoolteachers and politicians) showed their sympathy for the cause as well by joining students in boycotting Japanese goods and marching through the streets of China's major cities. Thanks to these multiclass mass actions, which reached their high point in the Shanghai general strike of early June, the Chinese government eventually yielded to the rising tide of popular indignation by giving in to two of the students' key demands: the warlord regime agreed to release most arrested activists from jail and dismissed from office the "Three Traitorous Officials" (the most despised members of the regime). In the wake of these events, the term "May Fourth" entered the Chinese vocabulary as a synonym for patriotic student activism.

The meaning of the term "May Fourth" goes much further than this, however, for over the course of the last seven decades, intellectuals and politicians have invested the date with additional significance. Because the protests of 1919 took place when Chinese students and professors were questioning traditional values and championing new conceptions of science and democracy, for intellectuals the term "May Fourth" also conjures up images associated with free thinking and a search for enlightenment. Last but not least, the CCP has attached its own special meaning to the term, by arguing that the intellectual and political ferment of 1919 led directly to the founding of the party. Thus, the year 1919 is said to mark the beginning of the "New Democratic Revolution" that eventually brought the CCP to power in 1949, and a bas-relief carving of May Fourth student protesters is accorded a prominent place on the Monument to the People's Heroes, which stands in Tiananmen Square, the symbolic heart of Beijing.

When students appropriated the symbolism of 1919 for themselves in the spring of 1989, giving speeches from atop the Monument to the People's Heroes and competing with official celebrations of the May Fourth anniversary, therefore, these acts did more than simply defy a few government regulations. They identified the students with a tradition linked to patriotism and enlightenment. This appropriation of the symbolism of May Fourth also posed a direct and powerful challenge to the CCP. If, as works by social theorists have convincingly shown, every government relies upon myths and rituals as well as guns and laws to justify and secure its rule, then it is fair to say that images and ceremonies associated with the May Fourth Movement play a crucial role in legitimating the CCP's power. When student protesters claimed the symbolism of 1919 for themselves in the spring of 1989 and implied that they (not the authorities) were the only true inheritors of the May Fourth tradition, the true representatives of May Fourth values, these youths challenged one of the CCP's most basic legitimating myths.

The targets of the prodemocracy protests of recent years have been well aware of just how serious a threat this kind of appropriation of May Fourth symbols can pose for the Communist Party. As a result, throughout the late 1980s, China's rulers have used various forms of propaganda to try to distance the newest generation of youthful protesters from the legacy of 1919. Thus, for example, since the May Fourth tradition has always been defined as patriotic and nationalist, the official press has tried its best in recent years to present prodemocracy protesters as unduly influenced by Western ideas and as the unwilling dupes of foreign manipulators. In addition, since both Chinese and Western historians characterize the mass actions of the May Fourth era as popular demonstrations with broad-based support, the CCP has frequently tried to portray recent protests as mere "riots" stirred up by "small groups of troublemakers" with secret agendas. Perhaps most damaging of all to the cause of campus activists, at least potentially, have been the attempts made by the party hardliners to link the present generation of student protesters to the Red Guards of the late 1960s, and thus tie contemporary activists to a very different tradition of youthful unrest than that identified with the heroes of 1919.

The Red Guards, who played so crucial a role in the early stages of the Cultural Revolution of 1966–1976, were in some ways quite similar to earlier generations of Chinese student activists. Like participants in the May Fourth Movement and other student struggles of the Republican era, the Red Guards staged classroom strikes and demonstrations, waged publicity campaigns to gain the support of the masses, and covered campus buildings with wall posters. In several crucial respects, however, the youth movement that accompanied the Cultural Revolution represented a departure from rather than an elaboration of the May Fourth tradition. Their intense personal loyalty to Chairman Mao, their blanket rejection of all aspects of Western culture other than Marxism, and their frequent use of violence to accomplish their goals—all set the Red Guards apart from participants in the great student-led mass movements of the Republican era. They themselves acknowledged this in their choice of role models, for the cultural heroes from whom the Red Guards most often traced their descent were not the students of 1919 but the Boxers of 1900.

Because of these special characteristics of the student protesters of the late 1960s, if CCP propagandists had been successful in their attempt to present the Democracy Uprising as nothing but a new form of Red Guardism, this would have directly undermined the efforts the students of 1989 had made to associate themselves with the May Fourth tradition. Moreover, since memories of the violence of the Cultural Revolution continue to haunt many Chinese of all classes, if the official propaganda campaign had succeeded it would also have alienated a great deal of popular support from the students. Chinese hard-line leaders had good reason to think that their effort to use the Red Guard legacy to discredit the Democracy Uprising in this way might work, in light of what had happened during the abortive prodemocracy struggle of two years before. Like the student protesters of 1989, the educated youths who took to the streets in the name of "democracy" (*minzhu*) in late 1986 and early 1987 had also attempted to link themselves to the May Fourth tradition by staging a protest on a key anniversary date—December 9, the anniversary of the second most famous Chinese youth movement of the Republican era—only to have school authorities and party officials respond by calling the protests the work of "New Red Guards." This propaganda, which struck a resonant chord both inside and outside the academic community among people still traumatized by memories of the "ten years of chaos," played an important role in undermining the prodemocracy movement of 1986–87.

In 1989, officials tried once again to tarnish the image of the Democracy Uprising by invoking images of Red Guard madness. The government press frequently referred to the student protests at Tiananmen Square as "turmoil" or "chaos" (*luan*), a term that in the political vocabulary of contemporary China has become a code word for the Cultural Revolution in much the same way that "democracy" and "science" serve as synonyms for May Fourth. In some cases hard-line propagandists took even more direct steps to link the students of 1989 to the Cultural Revolution, by speaking of the youths as "New Red Guards" whose supporters included remnant members of the "Gang of Four." These efforts to stir up negative memories of the "ten years of chaos" were aided by the fact that some of the tactics the students of 1989 used were indeed reminiscent of Red Guard actions. When youths in Wuhan and other cities descended upon provincial train stations en masse in the spring of 1989 to demand free passage to the capital, for example, though they were doing something that participants in the December Ninth Movement and other student struggles of the Republican era had been the first to do, some observers were bound to be reminded of events of the "ten years of chaos." Tactical continuities of this sort between the 1960s and the late 1980s were, moreover, by no means always mere coincidence. Though the student protesters of 1989 rejected the aims of the Cultural Revolution, they were undoubtedly influenced at times by the strategies their counterparts of the late 1960s had used. This was inevitable, since some of the younger professors and others who joined the students on the streets and advised them from behind the scenes had once been Red Guards.

In spite of all this, the government's attempts to use images associated with the Cultural Revolution to discredit the prodemocracy protests seem to have had done little to intimidate the students of 1989. Whether or nor this propaganda had an impact on the masses is harder to assess at this point. The massive outpourings of popular support that the Democracy Uprising received during April, May, and June suggest, however, that in 1989 the students, not the government, won the battle of historical analogies. The workers, teachers, journalists, and other urban residents who joined the students on the streets of various cities and in Beijing's Tiananmen Square showed by their actions that they at least believed the Democracy Uprising to be much more than mere *luan*, and that they were quite ready to accept the newest generation of youthful protesters as legitimate inheritors of the May Fourth tradition.

Historical Parallels and the Foreign Media

Western journalists covering the Chinese student demonstrations of 1989 routinely referred in passing to China's long history of student revolt and noted the existence of what I have been calling the May Fourth tradition. With a few notable exceptions, however, because of limitations of space (and in some cases also their own vagueness about Chinese historical events), these writers generally said little about the tradition other than that it existed, and that the first important Chinese student demonstration of modern times took place in the spring of 1919. Most newspaper and magazine articles thus left readers guessing what the significance of this fact was, or merely to dismiss the whole topic as a historical curiosity with little relevance for understanding contemporary events. This is unfortunate because, without more information, Western readers are likely to make three assumptions that will lead them to underestimate greatly just how important a role the May Fourth tradition has played, and will undoubtedly continue to play, in shaping the student protests of the last decades of the twentieth century.

The first faulty assumption readers are likely to make is that the May Fourth Movement was the only really significant struggle of its sort to take place before 1949. The truth is that the history of Chinese student movements stretches back at least as far as A.D. 156, the year several thousand scholars sent a mass petition of protest to the emperor to criticize instances of official corruption and injustice, and that many more student protests took place throughout the centuries separating that event from 1919. To cite but two of many cases, during the Song dynasty (960–1279) students staged a series of demonstrations and petition campaigns to call attention to official incompetence and threats to China's national sovereignty; and throughout the fifteen years immediately preceding the May Fourth Movement classroom strikes and student rallies were common features of Chinese academic and political life.

Students became even more active politically during the three decades following 1919. The experience of the May Fourth Movement convinced educated youths that they could and indeed should serve as the conscience of their nation, and surprisingly (at least to Westerners), workers and merchants frequently accorded students a right to speak out in the name of the Chinese people as a whole. Throughout the final three decades of the Republican era, with the exception of the period of the Japanese occupation of the early forties, hardly a year went by without some kind of popular agitation involving students taking place in one city or another.

Few of these Republican-era agitations grew into mass movements comparable to the May Fourth Movement in size and scope. The largest of them did, however, evolve into formidable affairs with important consequences for China's political development, and student movements played important (though often indirect) roles in precipitating the fall of the warlords in 1927 and the Nationalist regime in 1949. Like the May Fourth Movement itself, most of the great student-led struggles of the 1920s, 1930s, and 1940s, such as the May Thirtieth Movement of 1925 (in which workers and students shared the vanguard role) and the December Ninth Movement of 1935, were named for dates upon which foreign or native police forces interfered with patriotic demonstrations involving educated youths. Like the May Fourth Movement, these struggles usually began with students protesting abuses of power by Chinese officials, foreign threats to China's sovereignty, or most often some combination of the two. But, again like the May Fourth Movement, they all eventually expanded into battles over the right to protest itself. The events of 1919 also established a pattern that later student-led struggles tended to conform to quite closely in terms of the way these mass movements developed. The great youth movements of the 1920s, 1930s, and 1940s generally began with students in isolated areas staging demonstrations, drafting manifestoes and petitions, and forming first single-campus and then citywide protest leagues. As time went on, these movements grew to be national in scope and students began to solicit and receive support from workers and members of other social classes.

To sum up, far from being an isolated phenomenon, in terms of either form or impact, the May Fourth Movement was both the inheritor of a rich tradition of intelligentsia unrest and the progenitor of a whole series of Republican era mass movements. The students of 1989 were by no means the first educated youths to try to revive this May Fourth tradition during the period of Communist rule. Neither the popular protests that followed Zhou Enlai's death in 1976 nor the various short-lived waves of campus unrest of the mid-1980s evolved into national mass movements equivalent to the great student-led struggles of the

Republican era. These and other post-1949 protests, however, such as those that accompanied the Democracy Wall Movement of the late 1970s, incorporated and relied upon tactics and symbols associated with the events of 1919, and thereby helped to keep the May Fourth tradition of patriotic political activism alive.

The second faulty assumption Western readers are likely to make, besides thinking that the events of 1919 were unique occurrences, is to assume that four decades of CCP rule have made today's China a completely different country than it was during the warlord (1911–1927) and Nationalist (1927–1949) eras. We tend to think of Communist revolutions as totally transformative events, and in many ways Deng Xiaoping's China has become a very different place than that ruled by the warlords or by Chiang Kai-shek. There are, however, many other ways in which contemporary China is not so different from that of the May Fourth era. For example, it is still a nation where learning is revered and scholars respected, but also one in which the authorities are often intolerant of intelligentsia dissent. There are even more striking similarities between the present era and the years of Nationalist rule, the late 1940s in particular. Inflation, official corruption, one-party rule, an officially controlled press, government-sponsored youth associations claiming to be popular organizations—all of these things that today's students live with and protest against also angered their counterparts of the late 1940s.

The third faulty assumption Western (and particularly American) readers are apt to make about the Democracy Uprising is to think that the students of 1989 would have been more likely to find role models in contemporary events than in historical ones. This assumption comes from the likely association of campus unrest with the New Left protests of the 1960s. The American students who took to the streets to protest the war in Vietnam reveled in the idea that their generation's political commitment was unique. They generally had little interest in (and often seemed wholly unaware of) the fact that large strikes and demonstrations had taken place on U.S. campuses in the 1930s. When they looked for inspiration and models for action, they looked to the Civil Rights movement, contemporaneous protests by students in France and other countries, or Third World guerrilla struggles rather than to events that had occurred three decades previously and already seemed like part of a distant past. Given this background, it is easy to see why American readers would assume that Chinese youths of the 1980s would find more inspiration in foreign events like People Power or Solidarity's struggles than in student protests that took place in their country seventy years ago.

The problem with this reasoning is not that Chinese students are uninterested in what protesters in other parts of the world, and especially Asian countries such as South Korea, are doing. They undeniably are. The most obvious indication of this is that, while there are Chinese precedents for the group fasts that played so crucial role in the Democracy Uprising of 1989, hunger strikes of this sort were not a central component in the tactical repertoire associated with the May Fourth tradition. In this case, Chinese students were clearly inspired to a large extent by foreign role models, advocates of nonviolent resistance such as Gandhi and Martin Luther King, Jr. Nonetheless, throughout the Democracy Uprising, the students continued to be heavily influenced by the protests involving educated youths that took place in their own country in 1919 and other distant years. Such events are much more than things to be studied in history classes and then forgotten; rather, they are seen as part of an ongoing legacy with direct relevance for the students' own lives.

To understand why contemporary Chinese students remain so concerned with the actions of their precursors, it is crucial to remember that the CCP treats the history of the revolution less as an academic subject than as a religious one. The textbooks used to teach Chinese schoolchildren and college students alike invest key revolutionary figures (such as student martyrs) and events (such as the most famous student demonstrations of the Republican era) with a sacred significance. Yearly celebrations of anniversary dates such as May Fourth and December Ninth, which school authorities generally mark by holding special meetings or rallies and covering campus walls with posters commemorating student protests of the past, further glorify the revolutionary past. Other kinds of rituals also help keep the memories of this past alive in the hearts and minds of Chinese students. At Jiaotong University in Shanghai, for example, administrators encourage students to take part in ceremonies held during Qing Ming (the annual festival for the dead during which Chinese traditionally sweep the graves of their ancestors) at a shrine honoring two of the school's alumnae who were killed by the Nationalist authorities for taking part in the popular antigovernment protests of the late 1940s. At Tongji University, meanwhile, students are reminded to emulate their predecessors of the Republican era whenever they pass by their campus's special "youth movement history garden," one feature of which is a stream that runs the length of the park and symbolizes the passing of the May Fourth spirit from one generation to the next.

In this kind of environment, in which students are continually being reminded of and told to emulate the actions of the heroes of 1919 and 1935, it is hardly surprising that some students have invested the official lesson of keeping the May Fourth legacy alive with a radical activist meaning. Government speeches and proclamations issued on anniversary dates routinely claim that the best way for today's youths to follow in the footsteps of past protesters is to study hard and do all they can to help the CCP modernize the nation. According to this rhetoric, while it was right for these students to use demonstrations to try to save the nation when it was ruled by the warlords and the Nationalists, now that the CCP has saved the country from imperialism and given power to the masses, true patriots should work for stability rather than disorder. As the events of the late 1980s have shown, however, many of today's students have given a radical new interpretation to government calls for them to follow in the footsteps of the protesters of 1919 and 1935, by showing that they believe the patriotic goals of May Fourth and December Ninth remain unfulfilled and must be fought for on the streets.

1949 as a Dividing Line?

Throughout this chapter, I have stressed the continuities between past and present and the influence the May Fourth tradition had upon the participants in the Democracy Uprising. As important as the echoes of the pre-Communist past are for making sense of contemporary student unrest, however, two key differences between the student movement of 1989 and its Republican era predecessors should be noted here. First, China is now a much more independent nation than it was during the decades between 1919 and 1949. Throughout the warlord and Nationalist eras, imperialist threats of one sort or another frequently played a central role in motivating people of all classes to take to the streets. As a result, prior to 1949 a strong undercurrent of patriotic outrage influenced almost all Chinese protest activities, an undercurrent that led at times to acts of xenophobic violence. Though defenders of the May Fourth legacy tend to focus exclusively on the patriotism of the students and gloss over acts of this sort, it is worth remembering that in 1919 and other years, crowds did occasionally beat up foreign nationals or Chinese accused of being too friendly with the imperialists. In some cases, students of the warlord and Nationalist eras ostracized their classmates simply for wearing foreign clothes, believing in a foreign religion, or even dating foreigners. In contrast to this situation, imperialist aggression did not play a central role in motivating students to take to the streets in the spring of 1989, and from all reports the xenophobic underside of the May Fourth tradition had little impact on the Democracy Uprising, at least in Beijing.

Another major factor that makes the Democracy Uprising different from most of its Republican era counterparts is that there was no organized opposition party waiting in the wings in 1989, ready to help mobilize popular discontent and capitalize upon threats to the current regime's legitimacy. With the exception of the May Fourth

Movement, which took place before the founding of the CCP, underground Communist activists played at least some role in all of the great patriotic mass movements of the Republican era. Working as campus organizers, party members infiltrated school unions and tried (sometimes with little success) to channel student unrest to serve party goals. Before the Nationalists took control of the nation in 1927, their leaders also saw student discontent as a force to be used in their bid for power. In 1989, in contrast to say 1925 or 1947, there was no equivalent to these political parties to help give coherence and direction to popular anger. There was also no organization capable of presenting itself as a plausible successor to the CCP of Deng Xiaoping.

In spite of these and other contrasts between the contemporary struggle and the youth movements of the Republican period—for example, the unusually prominent role that members of China's ethnic minority groups, such as the student leader Wu'er Kaixi, played in the protests of 1989—it is the continuities rather than the breaks with the May Fourth tradition that remain most striking. In fact, when one looks more closely at some of the apparent dissimilarities, even they begin to seem less than absolute breaks with tradition. This is so, for example, in the case of the shift away from antiimperialist and antiforeign themes noted above. Though international relations were not a major issue in 1989, the students who took to the streets continued to speak of their mission as one of "national salvation" and to claim that they were the first and foremost patriots. In addition, while the Democracy Uprising itself was relatively free of antiforeignism, the xenophobic underside of the May Fourth tradition remains alive (if often muted) on China's campuses, as both the anti-Japanese demonstrations of 1985 and the anti-African disturbances of late 1988 clearly attest.

Patterns of Repression

As shown at the beginning of this chapter, many of the strongest parallels between past and present that emerged in 1989 relate to the techniques students used to express their anger and publicize their grievances. But there were also clear echoes of the past in many of the words and deeds Chinese officials used to suppress the Democracy Uprising. The Tiananmen Massacre may have been unprecedented in terms of the sheer level of carnage involved, but 1989 was by no means the first year in which a government had used brutal methods to suppress a Chinese urban mass movement. To cite but two of many relevant examples, members of the Western-run Shanghai Municipal Police force had fired into a crowd of unarmed students and workers on May 30, 1925. In 1947, at the height of the anti-hunger, anti–Civil War movement, the Nationalist regime launched a campaign of terror against students during which thousands of suspected activists were seized, hundreds of protesters were beaten, and troops fired into at least one school dormitory without warning.

Virtually every other feature of the CCP's drive to suppress the Democracy Uprising, besides the random violence of June 3 and 4, also had Republican era equivalents. The party's call for public meetings with specially selected student "leaders" in April 1989, for example, was reminiscent of the effort Chiang Kai-shek made over half a century before to undermine the December Ninth Movement by convening an almost equally contrived national student conference. When China's Communist rulers issued statements dismissing the popular protests of 1989 as the creation of a handful of troublemakers beholden to a foreign power, closed down newspapers sympathetic to the popular movement, imposed martial law to try to keep people off the streets, and organized obviously phony progovernment rallies to bolster support for their regime, they were once again using measures to which their counterparts of the first half of the century had turned.

These particular parallels with the past are especially ironic, since many of the top officials in charge of suppressing the Democracy Uprising began their political careers as student protesters during the Republican period. For example, both Qiao Shi

(Politburo member in charge of security) and Jiang Zemin (the Shanghai party secretary who rose to national prominence as Zhao Ziyang's successor as Deng Xiaoping's heir) were active in Shanghai youth movements of the mid- to late 1940s. Deng Xiaoping himself spent his youth working on underground student newspapers in France, activities for which he earned the nickname "Dr. Mimeograph." Even this irony of former protesters taking charge of suppressing renewed outbreaks of student unrest was nothing new in 1989, however, for the same thing occurred routinely during the Nationalist era. The case of Shao Lizi is one of several famous examples. Shao, who took part in one of the earliest Shanghai campus strikes in 1905 and then served as a key adviser to the student activists of 1919 and 1925, rose to prominence within the Nationalist regime after 1927 and went on to play important roles in government campaigns to contain new outbreaks of campus unrest.

Some Lessons from History

Having noted a variety of continuities and parallels between student movements of the Republican and contemporary eras, it is time to ask exactly how reference to the past can help to make sense of the Democracy Uprising and the Tiananmen Massacre. Looking to history for precedents is important and useful in this case for a number of reasons. As stated at the outset of this chapter, one reason is simply that we cannot hope to appreciate fully the meaning the students of 1989 themselves attached to their words and deeds without reference to the history of the student movement. Another reason is that the historical precedents help explain why students chose the specific methods they did for expressing their anger and seeking redress for their grievances. The students of 1989 were by no means mere imitators setting out to replicate the actions of earlier generations of Chinese youths, and some of their tactics were either innovatively original or adaptations of foreign protest techniques. Nonetheless, their shared knowledge of and attachment to the May Fourth tradition goes a long way toward explaining why certain familiar tactics figured so prominently in the Democracy Uprising.

Along with helping us to understand the tactical choices the protesters themselves made, looking to the past can also help us understand the view of the Chinese government toward the protests. Throughout the spring of 1989, from the very moment the marches marking Hu Yaobang's death began, the Chinese authorities consistently viewed the acts of student protesters as potentially important events. The same thing was true during the abortive prodemocracy struggle of 1986–87, which never succeeded in growing into a full-fledged mass movement. This is interesting because the rulers of other nations sometimes feel free simply to ignore equivalent manifestations of discontent by the educated youths of their own lands, as long as such demonstrations do not in and of themselves threaten the workings of the economy or the running of the state. Such is not the case in China, for the authorities are always aware that acts of popular discontent involving students need to be treated with the utmost seriousness.

Many factors that have nothing to do with the May Fourth tradition help to explain why the CCP fears student protests and takes the actions of educated youths so seriously. For example, despite the economic and cultural advances of the past decades, China remains a developing nation in which a relatively small percentage of people have received a college education, and for various reasons student movements tend to have a special power in countries where this is true. Nonetheless, it is impossible to understand fully the official response to the Democracy Uprising, to comprehend why the CCP's leaders feel so threatened by even the mildest of student protests, without remembering what took place during the first half of the twentieth century. As members of a party whose rise to power was aided by student-led mass movements, and in some cases as former participants in these movements as well, China's present leaders are intimately familiar with the ways in which educated youths have altered the course of China's history throughout the twentieth century. They are aware that student protesters helped to undermine the legitimacy of both the warlord and Nationalist regimes, by convincing Chinese citizens and foreign observers alike that these governments were corrupt, hypocritical, and generally unworthy to hold power. Party leaders are also well aware that, although student protesters themselves lack economic clout, throughout the Republican era China's educated youths managed to mobilize members of other classes, most importantly workers, whose actions had major consequences for the state's ability to function.

Unfortunately, the hard-line leaders who suppressed the Democracy Uprising learned only half of the lesson the history of Chinese student movements had to offer them. They learned that they had good cause to treat seriously the protests of educated youths. They seem, however, to have been completely oblivious to the equally important lesson the events of the Republican era hold: that although repressive campaigns of the sort launched in 1989 may succeed in the short run in limiting public dissent, they end up compounding instead of solving crises of legitimacy.

The most apt illustration of this concerns the events of 1947, for, as noted above, in that year, too, a Chinese government used violence and intimidation to put an end to popular manifestations of discontent. Though this campaign of terror succeeded in silencing Chiang Kai-shek's critics for a time, a mere two years later the Nationalist regime had finally and irrevocably lost its mandate to rule. Because of differences in the political contexts of 1947 and 1989, in particular the current lack of a powerful opposition party, history cannot tell us exactly what will happen next. The history of the past seventy years does, however, help confirm something political analysts have stressed ever since June 4: that the events of the spring of 1989 have created a legitimacy crisis that the CCP will not solve quickly or easily, if it is able to solve it at all.

Two

WHEN WORLDS COLLIDE: THE BEIJING PEOPLE'S MOVEMENT OF 1989

Tony Saich

THE SPONTANEOUS demonstrations that broke out in Beijing and other cities in the spring of 1989 were unprecedented in the history of the People's Republic of China. The size of the demonstrations and the depth of feelings the movement aroused rocked the Chinese Communist Party to its foundations and came close to bringing down China's orthodox leaders. The movement revealed an urban population that was deeply dissatisfied with the party's rule and very critical about the leadership's attempts at reform.

The initial seemingly confused reactions of the leadership and the subsequent crackdown demonstrated just how out of touch China's top leaders are with the processes of change that their own economic reform programs have set in motion. Key figures in the leadership have refused to see that the economic diversity and change had created new interests and groups in society that had to be accommodated by reforms of the authoritarian political system. Many saw the lack of political reform during the last decade as an essentially destabilizing factor. The movement and its brutal suppression were cruel proofs of this view.

This chapter is based on my article "The Rise and Fall of the Beijing People's Movement 1989," in *The Australian Journal of Chinese Affairs*, July 1990.

This chapter looks at the events within the broader context of the problems of spontaneous social movements within state-socialist contexts. Lack of sufficient information means that the focus is on the events in Beijing rather than throughout China as a whole. Although major demonstrations broke out in other urban centers, the movement began and effectively ended in Beijing. The occupation of Tiananmen Square, the symbolic center of Chinese Communist politics, meant that the struggle in Beijing became one for control of the nation.

Social Movements in a State-Socialist Context

The rise in spontaneous political and social movements in certain state-socialist societies over the last decade has created the need to reexamine some of the basic notions about political activity in such systems. Essentially, there was a general assumption that autonomous political and social movements that are a common feature of pluralist democracies cannot be tolerated in state-socialist systems. Such movements as do exist are mobilized by the regime for purposes of displaying large-scale support for policy decisions. By contrast, spontaneous movements are seen as undermining the ruling party's hegemonic position. Indeed, the ruling party has no mechanism to explain such a direct challenge to its "leading position" within state and society. The existence of an autonomous workers' organization, for example, directly challenges the ruling party's claim to represent the highest form of working-class consciousness. Such a clear challenge cannot be accepted, and the party will seek to crush the autonomous organization and denounce it as a "counter-revolutionary" organization.

Similarly, once the movement gains momentum, it is difficult to pursue any course other than one that will result in conflict. Strong emotions, once released, are notoriously difficult to bring back under control. The movement tends to develop a life of its own and often tends toward a fundamental critique of the state itself. If the state cannot see the necessity to redress the "just grievances" then there must be something fundamentally wrong with the state itself. The critique tends toward the moral and often assumes an iconoclastic form. The strength of the opinions held often closes off the solution of compromise through negotiation.

This highlights the key problem for nonsanctioned political and social movements in a state-socialist context. The political space in which they must act is extremely limited, and any noticeable increase in activity is liable to lead to confrontation. The capacity to develop is restrained by the fact that to expand they must confront highly centralized political institutions whose incumbents will repress or otherwise try to control collective action when it arises.

Such movements have been arising, however, with increasing frequency in state-socialist countries. Two factors are of importance: first is a conscious application by the regime of a policy of economic modernization and a subsequent downgrading of orthodox factors such as ideology and the all-embracing role of the ruling party. Second is the leadership's reaction to events.

It is generally assumed that there is a relationship between the level of socioeconomic development and the "sophistication" of the political system. Thus, with the exception of the People's Republic of China, recent movements have taken place in the Soviet Union and in the more economically advanced state-socialist countries of Eastern Europe that come more directly under the tutelage of Russia. Those states that have a less developed economy and that do not fall so directly under the Soviet sphere of influence have not experienced such large-scale disturbances.

A number of writers have suggested that as the imperatives of economic modernization come to the fore, pressure builds up for consequent reforms to make the system more flexible. Whether such pressures are responded to, however, depends on the party leadership. Simple economic development is not enough. Should the leadership respond, greater attention is paid to market mechanisms to regulate the economy and a larger role given to democracy, albeit for primarily functional reasons.

At this stage, however, a "participation crisis" is liable to occur.[1] Whereas previous participation had been predominantly "mobilized" for purposes of policy implementation and political socialization, the questions of autonomy, accountability, and interest representation are now placed on the agenda. Once such questions are broadly raised, the reaction of the party leadership becomes crucial. One choice is to move to crush all signs of the emergence of new sectoral interests and to try to reestablish party hegemony throughout all segments of society. The suppression of the Beijing People's Movement is merely the latest of such instances.

The example of Solidarity in Poland in the early 1980s suggests that mass support for change in the absence of support within the top party leadership will not result in change. Czechoslovakia in the late 1960s demonstrated that it is possible to have both the political will of significant parts of the party leadership and mass support for change without being successful. In the latter case, Soviet perception of interest proved decisive and it moved to thwart reform.

This has led many observers to interpret the chances of success for a political or social movement in terms of the strength of the ruling party at a given time. Where such movements thrived it was interpreted as a sign of regime weakness in terms of its ability to control the system totally. There are alternatives presented by regime weariness, however. One is for a movement to ally with sections of the political elite who also desire change. The chances of this strategy's success are greater when the "revolutionary" generation has passed from the scene. Leaders

---

[1]Donald E. Schulz, "On the Nature and Function of Participation in Communist Systems: A Developmental Analysis," in *Political Participation in Communist Systems*, ed. Donald E. Schulz and Jan S. Adams (Oxford: Pergamon Press, 1981), p. 30.

of the movement can seek to forge an identity of interest with a more technocratic, antibureaucratic group within the party.

Of prime importance is the attitude of the supreme leader in any particular state-socialist system, and of the leader of the Soviet Union in a system that comes under its sphere of influence. Mikhail Gorbachev has responded to the rise of sectoral interests in Soviet society by encouraging debate and accommodation— which has had an immediate effect on Eastern European attempts to seek reconciliation with civil society. It is highly improbable that the Polish communist authorities would have reached an agreement with Solidarity without the presence of Gorbachev in Moscow. Even the orthodox leadership in East Germany was forced to recognize the need for change with the exodus of skilled labor and the emergence of *Neues Forum*. While former leader Eric Honecker was able to retard the progress of demands for dialogue, the lurking presence of Gorbachev made some kind of move inevitable. The speed with which change came once Honecker was pushed aside, however, must have surprised even Gorbachev.

Attempts at accommodation do not mean that the ruling party will necessarily accept the emergence of a "pluralist" political system. Indeed, the party's actions are often intended to defend its privileged position of monopoly of power over state and society. The attempts at incorporation represent an attempt to prevent that plurality by revising the structure of the regime and the party's relationship to state and society.

Background to the Beijing People's Movement

The Beijing People's Movement must be understood in the context of the breakdown of the reform program from the mid-1980s onward. The frustration of key groups that had encountered major problems with the reforms explains why the student-launched movement was able to spread to other sectors of society and thus present the authorities with such a major challenge.

Since 1978, the leadership under Deng Xiaoping has tied its legitimacy more closely to its ability to deliver the economic goods than has any leadership since the founding of the People's Republic of China. As a result, key groups of technicians and intellectuals have been allowed greater freedom in return for their input into defining and implementing policies for economic growth. Thus, the leadership struck a number of tacit deals with key sectors of the urban society.

Intellectuals and students were offered a greater stake in China's future than had previously been the case. Measures were introduced to improve both their prestige and material conditions. However, the greater freedom to engage in academic debate was tempered by the need to stay within the wider parameters set by the party center. Problems arose with this system of regime patronage when the leadership divided and the guidelines were redefined in such a way that many of these "loyal intellectuals" now fell too far outside of the realms of the acceptable.

The dismissal of General Secretary Hu Yaobang in January 1987 following student demonstrations was a major turning point for intellectuals. Many saw Hu as supporting further experimentation with political reform and as the intellectuals' most important patron within the top leadership. Hu's dismissal was followed by the dismissal of three prominent critical party members and a short-lived campaign against "bourgeois liberalization." As a result, critical intellectuals began to question the validity of the tacit agreement. It seemed that the party could not be relied upon to keep its part of the bargain. Many of the harsh judgments that had been reserved for private discussion were thrown into the public domain.

Hu's "dismissal" also came as a shock for the students. After all, it was their demonstrations that had been used as the excuse to dismiss him. As the incipient elite, China's students had been offered a place of prestige in China's future in return for acquiescence to the party's overriding goals. What the party did not realize was that the students themselves wanted to play a major part in defining what that future would be. The two major rounds of demonstrations (December 1986 and April–June 1989) came after a perceived setback for the reformers. In particular, they should be viewed in light of the unfulfilled promises for political reform that had been presented by Deng Xiaoping himself as an important part of the reform program. The December 1986 demonstrations followed a summer of extraordinary debate in the official press on the need for a major shakeup of the political system. When China's top leaders withdrew to their summer retreat of Beidaihe, it was expected that they would draft a document on political reform. Instead, the published document stressed the need to combat "spiritual pollution," a war-cry of orthodox party leaders.

Thus, when the students took to the streets in December 1986, they did so with the intention of supporting what they perceived to be Deng Xiaoping's faction by giving renewed impetus to the need for greater political reform. Deng's hard-line reaction to these demonstrations and the dismissal of Hu opened the students' eyes to the fact that Deng was no true friend. Their belief in the capacity of the party to reform itself and significantly revise regime practice was thus undermined. This opened up the possibility for more radical activities.

The refusal to enter into serious political reform was compounded by the failure of the urban economic reforms and the declining position of the working class and state employees. Essentially, urban workers were offered a deal that involved giving up their secure subsidy-supported low-wage lifestyle for a risky contract-based system that might entail higher wages at the possible price of rising costs and unemployment. Many urban workers decided to reserve their judgment. Their reservation was exacerbated by the leadership's indecisiveness about urban reform, which resulted in a stop-and-go pattern throughout the 1980s. The insecurity mounted when the reforms after 1986 resulted in spiraling inflation without consequent improvements in material standards. Not surprisingly, talk of price reform and reduction in subsidies created a sense of panic. Zhao Ziyang's attempts to produce rapid economic results created the inflation of 1988 and 1989, which threatened those on fixed incomes. The resultant decline in living standards added many to the reservoir of urban discontent.

Urban anger was increased by the higher visibility of official corruption. Abuse of public positions and the privatization of public functions had reached extreme proportions by the late 1980s. Chinese society had become one "on the take" where, without a good set of connections and an entrance through the "back door," it was virtually impossible to participate in the benefits of economic reform. In this situation, the sight of children of high-level officials joy-riding in imported cars was a moral affront to many ordinary citizens. It was not surprising that the student slogan of "down with official speculation" (*dadao guandao*) found a large, enthusiastic audience.

By 1989, it was clear that in the eyes of many urban dwellers, the party's incompetence and moral laxness had eroded any vestigial notions that the party was a moral force in Chinese society. Once the students breached the dams, a flood of supporters was waiting to defend the students and attack the authorities.

The Students Take to the Streets

Three interrelated sets of issues are of relevance here: why, in particular, the students took up the challenge; how they organized themselves; and what kinds of issues they raised.

As in 1986, the student demonstrations must be seen in terms of a defeat for the reform program. The decisions taken at the National People's Congress (March–April 1989) made it clear that the then general secretary, Zhao Ziyang, and his proreform allies had lost the policy debate. Premier Li Peng and Vice-Premier Yao Yilin renewed the program of tight economic austerity that had been introduced in September 1988, but they now combined it with attempts to curtail political liberalization. The general malaise created by the reformers' defeat only needed a spark to convert it into a major expression of discontent.

This was provided by the death of Hu Yaobang on April 15. Whether true or not, the rumor that Hu's heart attack had come about while arguing the reformers' case at a Politburo meeting gave further impetus to the students' desire to demonstrate. On the evening of April 16 some three hundred students from Beijing University went to Tiananmen Square to lay wreaths in memory of Hu. The numbers began to swell as students from other colleges joined in. As with so many movements, a brush with authority gave the protests further impetus. On April 20, several thousand students had gathered outside Zhongnanhai, China's political nerve center, to stage a sit-in and had demanded that Premier Li Peng come out to talk with them. In a police charge, several students were injured. Official reports of the incident did not refer to student injuries but merely to "troublemakers" inciting the incident and wounding police agents. The episode supplied the students with the weapon of martyrdom, thus strengthening belief in their cause.

After the demonstrations began, it took about one month before other groups positively joined the students rather than simply offering passive support from the sidelines. Frank Niming analyzes in chapter 4 why other sectors of urban society did not join the demonstrations at an early stage. He outlines the high stakes of demonstrating and the extensive system of political control at the workplace.

The question remains, however, why the students took to the streets in such large numbers. Students in China form an elite group that could fully expect to take its place as the future power elite. Yet, unlike the critical intellectuals, the students had not been integrated into the system of regime patronage. As with students in many countries, they were alienated from their peer groups as well as from the mainstream of the party-dominated society. At the same time, although by no means well off, the students were not concerned so directly with the financial and social problems that beset the rest of Beijing's urban population. In addition, they were not subject to the same stringent outside controls as the other sectors of the population. This gave them the time and space to think more critically about China's future and to take risks that other sectors of society could not afford.

The rapid spread of the movement was facilitated by the fact that most students lived on campus, with the effect that news could spread quickly among them. Second, the close proximity of many campuses in northwestern Beijing made horizontal communications much easier. Thus, when external factors caused the students to organize, it was relatively easy for them to create a large-scale support movement in a short time. They could be guaranteed that speeches would be heard and strategically hung posters seen to maximum effect. Indeed, the campuses became focus points for sympathizers from off campus.

Student movements tend to be transitory phenomena, rising and falling quickly and unexpectedly. In part this can be accounted for by the relatively rapid turnover of student populations. What influences one generation does not necessarily affect the succeeding generation. Over the last ten years, however, China has been dominated by promises of political reform followed by the rejection of attempts to widen significantly the scope of political debate. Thus, the formative adolescent years of successive student generations have been dominated by the same themes. This has been compounded by the creation of a collective history of student activism that was passed from student generation to generation. The long-term points of reference are the patriotic movements of May Fourth (1919) and the anti-Japanese demonstrations of 1935 (see chapter 1). The short-term reference points are the student activism on campus since 1980. Staff members and graduate students living on campus provided a link with the recent past, thus providing an element of continuity that could substitute for persisting organizational structures.

The sporadic demonstrations throughout the 1980s provided the students with a learning process. In particular, they learned the need to link their particular grievances to broader problems within society. The government had been successful in portraying the 1988 student demonstrations as those of a spoiled, privileged group who had little to complain about. The nature of the slogans in 1989 meant that the government could not portray the movement in the same way.

While students were gaining practical experience through demonstrations, they were also developing on-campus activities. Lectures and "democratic salons" provided the students with the chance both to hear and to discuss unorthodox viewpoints. The later student leaders Wang Dan, Shen Tong, and Wu'er Kaixi all ran their own discussion groups. These on-campus activities were accompanied in early 1989 by a more radicalized atmosphere within Beijing's intellectual community at large. Of particular importance was the petition movement begun by Fang Lizhi's open letter to Deng Xiaoping (January 6) calling for the release of political prisoners. Fang and later signatories of the petition argued that the anniversary of the May Fourth Movement would provide a good opportunity for the release of Wei Jingsheng, who had been imprisoned as a result of the 1978–79 Democracy Movement.

With the heightened activity, the students began to organize themselves. Initially, this improved the capacity for action, but the eventual fragmented organizational structure made decision making cumbersome. Also, it hampered the students' capacity to act flexibly and decisively. Most important for galvanizing support was the development of links across the artificial, vertical divides imposed by the Chinese authorities. For example, it has always been difficult for workers to organize horizontally across the vertically organized, workplace-based official unions.

On April 18, students at Beijing University set up the first student autonomous organization. Students could nominate themselves for election, and eventually a leadership of nine was chosen. This was followed swiftly on April 20 by the formation of the first cross-college organization, the Beijing Students' Autonomous Federation (Beijing Gaoxiao Xuesheng Zizhi Lianhehui).[2] As the movement developed, this organizational unity began to fragment. On May 5, the College Students' Dialogue Delegation (Gaoxiao Xuesheng Duihua Daibiaotuan) was founded to formulate demands for discussions with governmental authorities. With the start of the hunger strike on May 13, the Student Hunger Strikers' Delegation (Xuesheng Juefantuan) was formed. Until the declaration of martial law and the termination of the hunger strike, these three organizations led the movement. In practice, the most influential of these organizations was that of the hunger strikers.

The hunger strikers were able to assume de facto leadership of the movement because of their moral authority. During the period of the hunger strike, when differences of opinion occurred between members of the three organizations, the opinions of the hunger strikers were deferred to. This was the case on May 18, for example, when certain members of the Students' Autonomous Federation suggested terminating the hunger strike. This was blocked by the majority of the hunger striker representatives. Organizational complexity was compounded by the arrival of many students from outside of Beijing. Indeed, it was the arrival of such students that gave the movement a further momentum in late May when many of the Beijing students were ending their activities. Major conflict arose about continued occupation of the Square. While key Beijing leaders proposed evacuation of the Square on May 30, the non-Beijing students rejected this. They proposed continuing the occupation until the proposed meeting of the National People's Congress began on June 20. The visiting students set up their own organization, the Autonomous Federation of College Students from Outside Beijing (Waisheng Gaoxiao Zizhi Lianhehui, or Waisheng Fujing Gaolian). By its very nature, the

---

[2] The federation was formally founded at a meeting on April 26 attended by some two thousand people, which elected a committee of seven.

organization's membership and structure changed from day to day.

The implementation of martial law forced the students to recognize the fractious nature of their organization. As a result, a meeting of students on May 23 decided to form a new organization with the ex–hunger strikers as its core. This was the seven-person Temporary Headquarters of the Student Movement (Linshi Xueyun Zhihuibu). The following day, the organization changed its name to the Headquarters to Defend Tiananmen Square (Baowei Tiananmen Guangchang Zhihuibu). This organization remained the most important until the end of the movement.

As the influence of the movement began to spread, nonstudent organizations were set up that complicated decision making even further. The two most important were the Beijing Intellectuals' Association (Beijing Zhishijie), headed by Zhao Ziyang's adviser, Yan Jiaqi, and the Beijing (or Capital) Workers' Autonomous Federation (Beijing [Shoudu] Gongren Zizhi Lianhehui). To accommodate these new groups, the Consultative Joint Committee of All the Capital's Groups (Shoudu Gejie Xieshang Lianxi Huiyi) was formed. This Joint Committee comprised five departments: the Supreme Headquarters, Propaganda Department, Liaison Department, Supplies Department, and Staff Department.

The presence of other organizations in the movement caused frictions with the students. Initially, to make criticism from the government more difficult, the students had sought to prevent other groups from becoming part of the movement. Even after the Workers' Autonomous Federation was set up, its headquarters was situated on the northwestern corner of Tiananmen, far away from the symbolic center of the students' movement around the martyrs' monument. Further, the Workers' Federation's open letter of May 21 must have offended the student leaders. It announced that as the "most advanced class," the workers should form the "backbone of the movement," and that its objective was to "lead the democratic movement." Indeed, Qiu Wu, the deputy commander-in-chief of the Workers' Federation, later claimed that after May 20, it was the Federation that became the most active in stopping the army vehicles from entering the Square rather than the students.

Unencumbered by years of experience within China's political system and not yet an integrated part of the power elite, the students could view the problems in simple, straightforward terms. Initially, the movement took on the appearance of a moral crusade with forces of good arrayed against a venal, unresponsive government. Students were perhaps the only group in society that could have made such claims and have them accepted by the wider society. With their stress on patriotism, the students appeared to many Beijing residents as a group less corrupt than any other in society. This role as the moral conscience of society was important in keeping the movement alive and drawing in broader public support. This moral image was heightened by the launching of the hunger strike on May 13.

Before the declaration of martial law and the embroilment of the movement in the party's power struggle, the students' demands offered simple solutions to complicated problems. Although there were specific demands related to the changing situation, essentially the students called for more democracy, freedom of the press, and an end to official corruption. Running throughout the movement were the appeals that the just and patriotic nature of the movement be recognized by the authorities, and that the latter open up a genuine dialogue with the students. At the beginning of the movement, the calls for reevaluation of Hu Yaobang, repudiation of the "anti–spiritual pollution" and "anti–bourgeois liberalization" campaigns, and correct evaluation of the present movement were calls for further political reform, while demands that the finances of leaders and their children be published addressed the question of corruption.

The focus on Tiananmen was, of course, no accident. The large square in the center of Beijing is the symbol of the authority of

Communist power. It was where the People's Republic of China was announced in 1949, and where all official rallies are held. By seizing the Square from the authorities, the students were making a frontal assault on the regime's legitimacy. Particularly with the massive demonstrations that began on May 15, it appeared as if it was the students who ruled Beijing while party leaders retreated into their bunker and looked on through binoculars.

This approach by the students made it difficult for the authorities to act. First, repression was unacceptable against a group that was demonstrating peacefully, singing the "Internationale," and calling for support of the CCP and further reforms and opening up. Yet, entering into dialogue would mean recognition of autonomous organizations in society, something that was anathema to orthodox party members.

With the hunger strike and the involvement of organizations that had close ties to Zhao Ziyang and the reformers, the demands of the movement began to change. From mid-May onward they became more directly political and sharply focused, a tendency that became much sharper after Zhao's defeat became obvious (May 19) and martial law was declared (May 20).

During the massive demonstrations that took place between May 15 and 18, slogans began to appear calling for Deng Xiaoping's and Li Peng's dismissal. Such calls, however, had not yet been sanctioned officially by the student leaders. Indeed, after the declaration of martial law, even though the demands and slogans became more pointed, caution still prevailed. Thus, on May 20, when the dialogue group announced its reactions to martial law, its call for the dismissal of Li Peng, Yang Shangkun, and Deng Xiaoping by a lawful meeting of the relevant organs was carefully premised on the fact that they had broken party regulations. Finally, aware that it was being sucked into the power struggle at the top, the delegation declared that it had no desire to become part of any factional struggle.

Notwithstanding this, the participation of other groups and the declaration of martial law inevitably pushed the movement onto a path of outright confrontation. At the demonstrations of May 22 and 25, slogans calling for the dismissal of hard-line leaders Li Peng, Yang Shangkun, and Deng Xiaoping as well as Beijing leaders Chen Xitong and Li Ximing had become commonplace.

This apparent radicalization and the participation of nonstudent groups frightened orthodox party leaders. Throughout the 1980s, they had been worried that a "Solidarity-type" situation might confront them. They clearly felt that tougher action was necessary. The participation of nonstudent groups provided them with the chance to convince fellow leaders that their earlier descriptions of the "sinister" nature of the movement had been correct.

The Government's Stumbling Response

While China's leaders recognized relatively early on the need to appear amenable to holding a dialogue with the students, the serious divisions among the party leadership prevented any real consideration of the students' demands. Also, considerations of individual power influenced the debates. Premier Li Peng and his supporters were fully aware that any form of concession to the students would mean the end of their political careers as well as opening up a Pandora's box of future demands.

The two main reactions within the leadership to the challenge posed by the students are linked to contrasting general views of the relationship between party and society: *traditional orthodox* and *pragmatic reforming*. These two viewpoints became polar points around which party members were forced to gravitate once the splits in the leadership could be contained no longer.

The traditional orthodox seek to run the party and its relationship to society along Leninist lines. Any effort to relax the party's grip over state and society is resisted, and means are continually sought to institutionalize party dominance. Unknown, unpredictable, and uncontrollable realities pose a threat to such a system. Pluralism in political life strengthens the unpredictability of social developments; therefore, diversity must be curbed, controlled, or channeled into very simple patterns of representation. Changes, if any, must be initiated by the center of authority and power.

This was shown in the response to the students' demands for dialogue. Until there was no alternative, leaders refused to acknowledge the existence of the autonomous student organizations and sought to channel all discussions via the officially sponsored student unions. Thus, on April 27 the government announced that it would talk with the *official* student organizations as long as the class boycott was ended. Similarly, demands for dialogue and recognition of the Students' Autonomous Federation on May 3 and 8 were rejected, although on May 8 the State Council and the National People's Congress did recognize the need for dialogue with the students. The talks that took place on April 29 and 30 were with the representatives of official student organizations.

This situation only changed with the start of the hunger strike on May 13. Government legitimacy would have been undermined even further if the students had been left to starve without any attempt at dialogue. Thus, visits and talks began, culminating in the televised meeting on May 18 between Li Peng and representatives of the hunger strikers. Li's stern response and lecture could hardly be termed a dialogue, however.

It seems that orthodox party members such as Li Xiannian, Chen Yun, and Wang Zhen saw the suppression of the movement both as a way to subdue the rising tide of dissent and as a way to remove Zhao Ziyang from his post as general secretary, thus paving the way for a major attack on his program of economic and political reform. Such orthodox leaders are aware that it is the economic reforms and the breakdown of traditional techniques of control that have provided a structural basis for the emergence of new forces in China, which they find difficult to accommodate within an orthodox Leninist structure. Their intention was to introduce a reign of terror, making their power visible to all members of the society. In launching the repression, they counted on the psychological exhaustion of the masses to undermine the emotional foundation of the protest movement.

In fact, this group had decided very early on the need to crush the movement. Their evaluation of the movement was dictated by their response to the student demonstrations of December 1986. In a talk on December 30, 1986, Deng Xiaoping supported the regulations to ban unauthorized demonstrations and suggested that student leaders who had organized the event should be arrested. He reiterated his view that stability and party leadership were essential for economic development, and that liberalization along Western lines for China was unsuitable. He put forward his support for the imposition of martial law in Poland and stressed that the move to maintain order would not damage China's reputation abroad.[3] In essence, his assessment did not change.

This previous assessment was repeated in the hard-line editorial in the *People's Daily* on April 26, which condemned the movement as a "planned conspiracy" directed against the party. The editorial, based on a speech of April 25 by Deng Xiaoping, claimed that the events were not a case of ordinary student unrest but a "political turmoil aimed at negating the leadership by the Communist Party and the socialist system."[4] It was supported by such orthodox veterans as Chen Yun, Li Xiannian, Peng Zhen, Yang Shangkun, and Wang Zhen. As was later acknowledged, this group of veterans effectively took over the decision-making process. Further evidence of the hard-line approach was the dismissal of Qin Benli, editor of Shanghai's proreform *World Eco-*

[3] "Main Points of Deng Xiaoping's Speech Concerning the Current Problem of Student Demonstrations," translated in "Party Documents on Anti–Bourgeois Liberalization and Hu Yaobang's Resignation, 1987," ed. James Tong, *Chinese Law and Government* 21, 1 (Spring 1988): 18–21. At a meeting of the Military Affairs Commission on December 25, 1986, some members had put forward the suggestion that martial law be implemented.

[4] This was mentioned in a secret speech by Li Peng at a meeting of senior leaders on May 22, 1989.

nomic Herald, on April 25, a day after the newspaper's issue calling for a complete reevaluation of Hu Yaobang was banned.

Despite the early decision to take a hard line, it took another six weeks before the protests could be crushed. Apart from the problem of using force against unarmed students, Zhao Ziyang came to oppose a tough response, favoring instead a limited dialogue.

It is important to note that the initial harsh decision was taken while Zhao Ziyang was in North Korea on an official visit. On his return, Zhao became aware of the popular support that the students enjoyed and proposed a change in tactics. He was particularly critical of the April 26 editorial. Zhao must have seen in the movement a chance to revive his own flagging political fortunes.

It might have been possible to resolve the crisis in a manner that could have given the party leadership under Zhao Ziyang a new lease on life, allowing it to place itself at the head of a new spirit of national unity. The student movement was similar to that of Burma in that, while it had morally impelling demands, it had no precise program or idea of how to reach its objectives. In the absence of concrete proposals on how to reach those objectives, the party could have offered its own minimal agenda, which might well have been enough to satisfy the majority of demonstrators and still left the party firmly in control of the political system. An offer to allow a couple of independent newspapers, a quasi-autonomous student federation, and freer elections to the NPC, while marking a noteworthy change, would not have undermined the party's leading role. Further, it would have given a clear signal that party leaders were aware that the world they ruled over was in a state of change.

On May 3 and 4, Zhao made two important speeches that seemed to indicate at least tacit support for the students' aims. On May 3, commemorating the seventieth anniversary of the May Fourth Movement, although calling for political stability, Zhao did not include the need to "oppose bourgeois liberalization" in his speech. The insertion of this phrase had been requested by Li Peng and various other "comrades."[5] When talking to Asian Development Bank delegates on May 4, Zhao claimed that China was politically stable and that the "reasonable demands of the students should be met through democratic and legal means, through reforms and various other means in line with reason and order." According to Li Peng, this speech had not been approved by any other member of the Standing Committee of the Politburo.

In contrast with the orthodox leaders' attempts to suppress media coverage of the movement, Zhao saw such coverage in a favorable light. Major press coverage was given to his speeches and to the demonstrations that had taken place on May 4. Importantly, a group of three hundred journalists from party-controlled papers joined the demonstration to call for greater press freedom. While there is no direct evidence that they were prompted by Zhao's supporters, at a meeting on May 6 with Zhao's allies Hu Qili and Rui Xingwen, who were in charge of propaganda and ideological work, Zhao suggested that there was "no big risk" in reporting the demonstrations and in increasing the openness of the news.

As a result of Zhao's speeches and actions, it became clear to all that the party leadership was severely divided. This made it safer for nonstudent groups to participate in the demonstrations. Journalists, encouraged by Zhao's response, on May 8 called for an end to censorship. The following day, over one thousand people from thirty official news agencies agitated for greater press freedom.

From May 15 to 18, Beijing witnessed enormous street demonstrations joined by all sectors of society. The moral appeal of the hunger strikers, the loosening of reporting restrictions, and attempts by pro-Zhao work units to pressure his opponents brought ever greater numbers of citizens out onto the streets.

---

[5]Mentioned by Li Peng in his speech of May 22, 1989.

Between May 11 and 13, Hu Qili, Rui Xingwen, and Yan Mingfu, together with the more orthodox head of the Propaganda Bureau, Wang Renzhi, met with representatives from key media organizations and informed them that people should know about and discuss important matters, while problems should be resolved in a democratic and legal manner. On May 15, Zhao and Hu Qili expressed their understanding of the journalists' complaints and demonstrations and called for an opening up of the press.

Similarly, pro-Zhao intellectuals and organizations started to lobby on his behalf. Intellectuals became more outspoken in their criticisms. On May 13 a poster written by proreformers appeared at Beijing University urging intellectuals to take part in the demonstrations. On May 14, twelve prominent intellectuals issued an appeal on the current situation, saying that they would join the hunger strike if the movement was not termed patriotic. On May 16, they set up the Beijing Union of Intellectuals. On May 17, Yan Jiaqi and Bao Zunxin, among others, signed a manifesto demanding the abolition of the dictatorship, reaffirming that the movement was patriotic. They claimed the movement would lead to the destruction of the dictatorial and autocratic regime.

On May 19, Zhao's supporters made a direct appeal to use the movement to oust his opponents. Four organizations close to Zhao met under the chairmanship of Chen Yizi, director of the Economic Structural Reform Institute, and drafted a six-point statement. Their pamphlet, which was read out on the Square and distributed widely, demanded that the "inside story of the decision making of the top leadership and the divergence of opinions" be made known, and that special sessions of the NPC and the Party Congress be convened. It also urged the students to "end their hunger strike as soon as possible," hinting that the government would otherwise adopt military measures to control it. The statement laid the blame for the situation on the party, claiming that never before had it been so isolated from the masses.

While this mobilization was taking place, however, Zhao was losing the struggle within the party. Two meetings settled his fate, and ultimately that of the citizens occupying the square. The first was held at Deng Xiaoping's home and was attended by Zhao Ziyang, among others. Deng referred to the deep divisions in the leadership but stated that these would not be discussed at the meeting: the only issue was martial law. The general consensus was that retreat was impossible, but Zhao expressed his disagreement with the policy. It is important to note here that the decision to implement martial law was taken not by a formal party body but by an ad hoc meeting following discussions between Deng and other veteran party leaders.

At 8:00 the same evening, a meeting of the Standing Committee of the Politburo was held to ratify this decision. Zhao again expressed his opposition and announced that he wished to step down as general secretary. Zhao's objections were swept aside, and the decision to implement martial law was ratified.

This explains Zhao's pathetic appearance when he came to the Square on the morning of May 19 to ask the students for forgiveness, saying that he had come too late. That night, Li Peng announced that sterner measures would be introduced to control the situation in the capital. At 10:00 the next morning, he signed the declaration of martial law for strategic areas within Beijing. On May 22, Premier Li and President Yang Shangkun addressed a secret meeting of top party leaders to rally support for martial law; to pave the way for Zhao Ziyang's removal;[6] to restore Deng Xiaoping's position as China's supreme leader and to prepare party and army members for the suppression of the democracy movement. The world of the Beijing People's Movement collided with that of the orthodox party leaders resulting in the brutal suppression of June 3 and 4.

---

[6] Yang Shangkun, in a speech on May 24 to an enlarged emergency meeting of the Military Affairs Commission, made it clear that the decision to remove Zhao from his posts had already been taken.

Concluding Comments

The rise and fall of the Beijing People's Movement confirms some of the general trends outlined earlier. The stress on economic modernization since 1978 and the resultant social developments were beginning to produce a more differentiated society that the party was finding increasingly difficult to dominate. In this respect, it is noteworthy that two of the students' main support groups came from the newly flourishing private sector. First, there was the Flying Tiger Motor Brigade, which provided the students with their information about troop movements after martial law was declared, and which was able to spread student information throughout the city. It is no surprise that the first arrests (May 30) were of members of this group. Second, there was the Stone Computer Company, which was instrumental in terms of both financing the students and providing them with advanced communications networks.

The absence of a consequent development of political institutions that would moderate and channel conflicts led to calls for a speedier pace of reform. The refusal of the party to revise its relationship with society and to develop new, effective political institutions meant that activities became increasingly antisystemic.

As in many other developing countries, the greatest challenge to the established system was mounted by the students. Their freedom from the constraints that trap other groups of urban society and their relatively simple analysis of the problems led them to launch the movement. In this respect, the movement differed from that of Poland, where the actions of the working class played a dominant role. Over the short term, the fact that the backbone of the movement was composed of students was a strength making it difficult for the authorities to react. Over the long term, however, the inability and perhaps even unwillingness to forge links with the working-class participants proved a weakness.

As with many movements, the Beijing People's Movement

began to take on a life of its own. The vacillation of the authorities, followed by the increasingly apparent division in the top leadership, encouraged the students to forge ahead. The students, convinced of the moral righteousness of their position, were not willing to compromise. As the movement progressed and other groups joined in, it was clear that many grievances that had been suppressed for decades were beginning to erupt into the open. This had already occurred months earlier in the pro-independence demonstrations in Tibet.

Unlike in the Soviet Union, where Gorbachev has maintained a majority within the party leadership that accepts that such long-term grievances can no longer be suppressed, Deng Xiaoping decided to throw his weight behind those who favored repression. Thus, in both Tibet and Beijing, martial law was implemented and force employed. In part, the tough approach in China can be explained by the persistence of the revolutionary generation of leaders in key positions of power. Clearly, the veteran leaders have retained key decision-making power in the Chinese political system, undermining the official stress on the institutionalization of Chinese politics and the idea that an orderly succession can be achieved.

The movement and its suppression has left the Chinese political system extremely unstable. The current leadership must rule without the active support of key sectors of its urban population. As a result, it has little choice but to deal harshly with future unrest. The leadership has now alienated successive student generations who have grown up in the atmosphere of reform. Many of those who demonstrated in the past did so thinking that they were supporting the party policy of reform and opening up. The students will have learned from the failure of peaceful revolution. Further, with the purge of Zhao Ziyang and his supporters, there is no group at the top of the party that can take over the reformers' mantle. This means that an important part of the necessary dialogue and opinion stream is shut out of the debate. In turn, the lack of sympathizers at the top means that, instead of dialogue, further conflict can be expected.

The problems for the leadership are further compounded by Deng Xiaoping's desire to continue with the economic reforms. Here a dilemma arises. Continued reforms in the economic sphere will bring with them the same political problems with which the current leadership has refused to come to terms. China's current leaders share the views of the nineteenth-century reformers. To both groups, technology is essentially neutral, something that can be grafted onto any socioeconomic system. They refuse to see the link between technology and the socioeconomic matrix that has produced it. Ironically, they have the un-Marxist view that change in the economic base does not imply change in the political superstructure. Their idea that the social and political implications of the economic program can be stopped by launching campaigns of ideological education is a nonstarter. Sooner or later, the party will have to come to terms with the implications of its own desire for economic growth. Unless it does so swiftly and in a manner that creates a real forum for dialogue among the different interests in Chinese society, the party risks being swept away by a further round of social unrest. Its only alternative would be further warfare on its own people.

Three

THE POLITICAL ECONOMY BEHIND BEIJING SPRING

Kathleen Hartford

IT IS HARD to feel sympathy for dictators with blood on their hands. It is all the harder if we have lived and laughed, hoped and dreamed, with their victims, as so many of us did while the Beijing spring movement unfolded. And having had the dubious privilege of watching the dictators' fist come down, we feel that this is an act whose brutality is matched only by its insanity. Nothing, we think, can justify this; nothing, we thus conclude, can explain it. There can be no sympathy for the devil.

But the dynamics that were so tragically played out around Tiananmen are in fact quite explicable. For there are larger, longer-term, and underlying causes of the recent—and on-going—Chinese tragedy, which will continue to bedevil the Chinese body politic, and *any* leadership group it might produce, until those causes are themselves correctly identified and addressed. The causes are located in the rapidly changing political economy during the decade of reforms of the Maoist-Stalinist system that began at the end of the 1970s. As I will argue in this essay, the reform project has run aground on two dilemmas. It is only the convergence of these dilemmas—of socialist reform and of politico-economic development strategy—that can explain, on one hand, the intensity and breadth of the mass movement of spring 1989, and, on the other hand, the first dithering and then ferocious response of the CCP leadership.

50

The program of economic reform is in deep trouble, and it had been for some time before the mass movement emerged. Part of the problem has been political and ideological opposition from those among the party leadership who think the reforms have gone too far in undermining the bases of China's socialist system. One further part of the problem is that corruption among officials has seemed to grow geometrically as the economy has grown arithmetically. Eliminate both those causes, however, and the basic dilemmas for the economic reforms would remain. The easy stage of economic reform has concluded; the long, hard, painful stage has begun, and every measure aimed at pushing the reforms along threatens also to undermine them—and the power and legitimacy of the Communist government—fatally.

Why should this be the case, when reforms had begun with such promise and popular support? We must keep in mind here that the reform of any socialist system is a complex process. Socialist reform, in general, has meant the task of transforming a command-planned, highly centralized system under public ownership into a market-oriented, decentralized, mixed ownership system. In the Chinese socialist system in particular, reform would affect both an urban sector dominated by state-owned industry and a rural sector in which collectively owned and managed farms organized production and controlled output. In addition, Chinese reform would have to be aimed at the mechanisms of the state's allocation of inputs, setting of output quotas, determination of prices for virtually all products, control of almost all commercial channels, monopoly on credit and foreign exchange, and a host of other means used to enhance central state control over economic activity.

In addition to these tasks, because of the political and economic variations on socialism introduced under Mao Zedong, particularly (though by no means exclusively) during the decade of "Cultural Revolution," reform in China has meant as well the attempt to transform political power-holders' style of wielding power. Mobilizational methods, "campaign" pushes, political interventions in economic management, and arbitrary use of power were to be changed to a style guided by principles of legality (and legal accountability), separation of economic management and political decision making, and general institutionalization.

The first, more general type of socialist reform appears to be largely economic in character, while the more peculiarly Chinese task of reform appears largely political. However, the ways in which polity and economy have been intricately intertwined and articulated over the past forty years make it impossible to define either task as purely economic or purely political. The interrelatedness of the tasks of reform has been highlighted with each concrete step taken on the reform road.

The Rural Reforms

The reform process began with the rural areas, partly because failures in the agricultural system under Mao were seen as underlying causes of China's general economic problems at the end of the 1970s, and partly because the rural sector was easier to reform. Despite the collectivized agricultural system, there was a minimum of bureaucratic opposition and a promising maximum of political support (from 800 million peasants). This was taking place in a context where the new leadership had to cultivate a base of support quickly.[1] Rural reform developed in two somewhat overlapping stages, the first running roughly from 1978 to 1984; the second, from 1984 to 1988.

In the *first stage*, reform policies focused primarily on reforming producer incentives to elicit increases in rural output, and to effect some changes in the composition of rural production. Three principal types of measures were used. The first was mar-

---

[1]Information on the rural reforms is drawn from my manuscript under revision, *Dilemmas of Socialist Reform: Rural Development and Food Policy in China, 1978–1989*, for the Harvard Council on East Asian Studies Publications.

ket liberalization, including expanded freedoms for peasant households to produce for the market. This process began as early as 1977 in some areas but was in full swing by the beginning of the 1980s. The state reduced somewhat its stranglehold on the purchases of rural produce, eventually permitting collective farms and peasant households to sell excess quantities in free markets (where prices were generally much higher) once they had satisfied their state purchase quotas. The state monopoly on retail sales of food grain was relaxed. Local authorities began to encourage the opening of new rural and urban markets, rather than prohibiting them as in the "Cultural Revolution" era, and such markets proliferated and their sales boomed. Some collectives and individual peasant entrepreneurs began long-distance trading to take advantage of the new market opportunities.

The second type of first-phase rural reform was in state extractive measures. Producer prices for farm products had been held low for decades, while compulsory sales to the state rose with increases in productivity. In effect, this arrangement extracted resources from agriculture to fund industry and urban economic growth. But it also discouraged agricultural production. In 1979, the CCP Central Committee announced the first in a series of purchasing price increases and tax and compulsory sales quota reductions. The cumulative result of these changes was that by 1984, the average state purchasing prices of grain, cotton, and oilseeds had risen by 50 percent, while the prices of some other major products had risen even more.[2]

The third and most highly touted of the first-phase rural reform measures was the introduction of contractual "responsibility systems." These eventually restored household farming and paved the way for a formal end to the commune system (though not to state and collective control over use of farmland). House-

---

[2] Unless otherwise indicated, statistical data in this paper are drawn from the statistical yearbook series compiled by the State Statistical Bureau. These issues are available in both Chinese and English editions.

hold contracts were introduced experimentally in some of China's poorest rural areas at the end of the 1970s, and by the early 1980s they began spreading nationwide, sometimes as a spontaneous surge from the peasants, sometimes (especially in more highly modernized areas where collective agriculture had been rather successful) in grudging compliance with fiats from above. By 1984, 99 percent of the rural production teams reported using comprehensive contracts for farmland that left peasant households in control of their own surplus after making their share of compulsory deliveries to the state and their required lump-sum payments to the collective farm. Later regulations guaranteed ten- to twenty-five-year contracts for land use to peasant households and permitted the inheritance of these contracts.

With this reorganization of the basis of agricultural production, many of the previous functions of the institutions that had managed collectivized production became defunct, while others (such as provision of technical services and guarantees of state purchasing targets) remained important. In the hope of rationalizing organizational systems in the countryside, the national leadership decided to separate governmental and economic functions at the local level. New township (*xiang*) governments replaced the political role of the old communes, while new specialized bodies known by a variety of names (associations, cooperatives, companies) performed on contract basis the technical or special functions hitherto performed by brigades and communes. Moreover, aside from farmland, which was still largely reserved for collective ownership, private purchase of agricultural and non-agricultural means of production in rural areas was not only permitted but encouraged. Many peasants purchased their own trucks and tractors; some set up livestock farms, warehouses, workshops, and factories.

As the foregoing descriptions suggest, the emphasis during the first phase of rural reform was placed on improving incentive systems so as to increase production. An additional emphasis, however, was the diversification and restructuring of rural economic activity. Diversification was intended partly to raise incomes more rapidly, partly to soak up the 30 to 50 percent of rural labor that was estimated as "surplus." It was avidly pursued by both collectives and individuals. Many households, and even entire regions, began to specialize in crops other than grain, or in poultry production, or in aquatic products, or in myriad other agricultural and nonagricultural pursuits.

The successes of the first phase of rural reform wrought such enormous changes in the rural economy that by 1984, a second phase of reforms began to emerge. In this second phase, the reform process had two main emphases: "commercialization" and "specialization" (with both domestic and international trade implications) of the rural economy, and rapid development of industrial and other nonagricultural enterprises in rural areas. The combination of these two emphases emerged as the foundation for an increasingly self-conscious strategy for continued rural development. Such a strategy became all the more necessary as rural producers utilized nearly all the previously unused capacity or latent productivity, and new sources of productivity had to be created.

The emphasis on commercialization meant that future increases in productivity and income depended on increasing engagement in "commodity production," or production for sale rather than for own use. Increasingly, however, it also came to mean orientation toward market signals as the indicators of what and how much to produce.

If any one vehicle was most likely to promote, and realize the benefits of, commercialization, it was the "specialized household." Specialized households comprise "peasants" who use most of the family labor power in one line of production, make relatively high capital investments, employ relatively advanced technology, and sell most of their production either to the state or on the free market. They were considered so important as a model for further rural development (and as a mechanism ensuring that the state could meet its procurement targets) that they were given preferential access to credit and scarce inputs, and often first crack at procurement contracts when those were hard to come by. Local Communist Party cadres' performance in developing specialized households was made one of the chief criteria in the rural party rectification pursued in 1984 and 1985.

Not only households but whole regions were exhorted to attend to commercialization as the route to rural development. In areas close to urban centers, this meant orienting production toward the urban consumer market. In coastal areas with appropriate conditions, it meant orientation toward foreign markets. In Guangdong Province, some farms formed contract joint ventures with Hong Kong companies for pig production. Some parts of Liaoning Province contracted with multinational agribusiness companies to produce fruits and vegetables for the Southeast Asian market.

The emphasis on commercialization received a big boost—perhaps, in hindsight, rather too big a boost—from the decision, announced as 1984 slid into 1985, dramatically to revamp the state commercial system for agricultural produce. This was to transform the mandatory planning system for agriculture, with its imposed sales quotas at fixed prices, into a system of voluntary contractual sales at prices shaped by market forces. As announced by Zhao Ziyang in January 1985, the new policy meant, for rural areas, limiting the amount of produce purchased by the state (which previously had attempted to buy everything peasants were willing to sell) and allocating the sales by advance contract. For the cities, it meant releasing prices of farm products other than grain to reach market levels (with, however, wage subsidies to cushion against the anticipated price increases). Thenceforth, supply and demand as indicated through market prices would guide the decisions of rural producers, who could choose to produce either for the state or for the free market. The big exception was grain, which was considered too vital a part of national food supply and of nutritional needs to leave entirely to market mechanisms. The producer price was held low (not terribly low in 1985, but increasingly so thereafter); the consumer retail price was held even lower; and subsidies by central and local governments made up the difference.

In this situation, grain production was not a very attractive proposition for most farmers. The proposed solution was to "concentrate" land for grain cultivation in the hands of specialized farmers who possessed special skills and could make large-scale grain cultivation a profitable pursuit (and who would, incidentally, probably have to sell most of their output to the state if they wanted a steady market or access to cheap fertilizer, credit, and diesel fuel). Other farmers would presumably voluntarily hand over the contracts on their land, in return for cash or grain, and take the opportunity to engage in some line of activity more lucrative for their own skills.

But where? Here enters the second major emphasis of the second-phase rural reforms, the development of rural nonagricultural enterprises, both collectively and privately owned. Already during the late Maoist era, under a local/regional self-sufficiency strategy, rural industries and other nonagricultural enterprises had begun to grow rapidly. Now, however, with the emphasis on commercialization that encouraged interregional and even international linkages, rural enterprises took off into a new era of growth. This was helped by generous provisions of credit, tax holidays, and other incentives from local and national governments, and by investments and technical assistance from urban and international industries subcontracting to the rural enterprises. Not only manufacturing industries, but also transport, construction, and a wide range of service enterprises developed. By the end of 1988, these nonagricultural pursuits produced over 53 percent of the total value of rural output, as compared to 31 percent in 1980.

The aggregate results of the rural reforms were in many respects extremely impressive. In value terms, agricultural output grew at an average of 6 percent per annum from 1979 to 1987. From 1980 to 1987, the gross output value of agriculture grew by 143 percent, while the gross output value of all other rural economic activity rose by 446 percent. Peasant incomes rose at a dizzying rate, with per capita income averaging 134 yuan in 1978, 355 yuan in 1984, and 545 yuan in 1988. The value and income figures are in nominal rather than real terms, and the unreliability of official price indexes and sampling procedures is well known; therefore, the numbers must be discounted to some undetermined extent. The fact remains that the real increases are tremendous.

That much is clear from the data on increased production and consumption. From 1978 to 1988, grain production rose a total of 29 percent by physical volume; cotton, by 94 percent; oilseeds, by 154 percent; meat, by 155 percent; and sugar crops, by 162 percent. Such jumps in production made possible large increases in food consumption in both urban and rural areas. Nationwide, in just ten years from 1978 to 1987, the average per capita consumption of grain went up nearly 30 percent; that of pork, nearly 90 percent; sugar and confections, nearly 100 percent; and alcohol, over 300 percent. The quality and variety of food products in cities improved rapidly. By the late 1980s, free markets in major cities offered a virtual cornucopia of foods even in the depths of winter.

Lurking behind such good news, however, there are serious problems. The benefits of rural development have been far from equally distributed, particularly as the chosen strategy and attendant allocation of resources since 1984 have favored the already more highly developed coastal and suburban areas. As for many of those in poorer areas, and for a small percentage of those even in better-off areas, it is now recognized that incomes have actually fallen in real terms. And while the total number of those who are malnourished has decreased, the incidence of serious malnutrition appears to have increased.

Rural poverty is no longer a problem solely for rural areas, for the reforms have provided opportunities for peasants to seek employment elsewhere. This they have done in droves. By late 1988, there were an estimated 50 million "transients" in Chinese cities. The numbers would seem to have increased dramatically in 1989. Migrants from the impoverished Northwest and Southwest poured into Guangzhou [Canton] and the Pearl River Delta by the hundreds of thousands after Chinese New Year 1989. By March, it was reported with some alarm that the flood of migrants was even reaching Hainan Island, some 200,000 such migrants having been counted. In one day alone, some 14,000 arrived at Haikou. Some 450,000 migrants were reported in Beijing in May.

The population movements evoked strong—or perhaps one should say intense—government responses. Local authorities first pleaded with migrants to return home, then resorted on occasion to forcible removals. The State Council issued an urgent circular to all provinces, municipalities, and departments, to "do a good job in strictly controlling the blind outflow of laborers." Yet, the farmers from poorer areas continued to vote with their feet.

Compared to the looming grain problems, all of this may be only a minor irritation for China's leaders. The country's output of grain, still the major source of calories and protein for 1.1 billion Chinese, has essentially stagnated since 1984, while population growth rates have accelerated. The major reason for the stagnation is that grain pays much less than other crops or than nonagricultural activity. Therefore, those farmers with money to invest have tended to put it into nongrain crops or into nonagricultural activities. Much farmland has been abandoned, and much more has deteriorated rapidly as the water conservancy system formerly funded by collectives and local governments falls into disrepair. Even those who grow grain increasingly tend to grow only enough to feed themselves.

Moreover, the grain that is available is increasingly difficult for state procurement agencies to acquire. In 1988, the state ran out of cash for its procurement of grain and other crops and eventually succeeded in purchasing enough grain to feed the cities only by issuing IOUs (many of which were still not redeemed when farmers had to begin planting in 1989), and by using various subtle and not-so-subtle forms of coercion to force peasants to sell. Violent and sometimes armed resistance to state tax collectors and procurement agents was reported from a number of rural areas.

The marketed grain shortage has been made up partly by increasing imports, which reached some 15 million tons in 1988. It is conceivable that China could import much more, but only at the price of vulnerability to sharp price shifts in the world market, not to mention possible political use of the "food weapon" by one or more of the major grain-exporting nations. Indeed, as discussion of urban reforms will show, the money may not be there to pay for imports.

The Urban Reforms

Urban industrial reforms got off to a considerably slower start than rural reforms.[3] Experiments with reform of urban state-owned enterprises began in 1979, and some relaxation of central government controls started early in the 1980s. It was not until the fall of 1984, however, that the reformist leaders felt confident enough, and more conservative leaders willing enough, to announce the start of a concerted, nationwide reform of urban enterprises and the state-planned urban economy.

---

[3] Information on the urban reforms other than that available through primary sources is based primarily on the work of Andrew Walder and of Yves Chevrier; on the major article by Hua Sheng, Zhang Xuejun, and Luo Xiaopeng, "Ten Years of Reform: Review, Reflection and Prospects," *Jingji yanjiu* (Economic Research), no. 9 (September 1988), translated in *JPRS*-CAR-89-004, January 11 1989, pp. 16–45; and on a manuscript by Frank Niming, *Op het scherp van de snede: Achtergronden en Ontwikkeling van de Chinese Volksbeweging 1989* (On the Knife's Edge: Background and Development of the Chinese People's Movement 1989) (Kampen: Kok-Agora, forthcoming).

Reforms in the urban sector have had four major characteristics: decentralization, marketization, intensification of incentives, and internationalization. Perhaps it should be said that these have been the intentions of the reforms, but not always their results.

Decentralization began with experiments in Sichuan in 1979, whereby central ministries' direct controls over individual enterprises were increasingly relaxed. The initial basic idea of this decentralization was to free enterprises from the restrictions of central state controls over the distribution of profits (previously profits had to be handed over in toto to the central ministries), although they were still held to central state plans. Later decentralization measures devolved planning responsibilities and a large chunk of the profit distributions, for all but the most basic industries, to provincial or local-level authorities.

Although most Chinese sources tended to view this shift as part of an ongoing process of decentralization right down to the enterprises, some observers suggested that it constituted in practice an intensified centralization (of control of inputs and output and therefore of enterprises' economic decisions), though at a lower level of administration than previously. Indeed, the increase in power and economic resources that devolution put into the hands of local authorities seems to have revivified and strengthened local "relationships" (*guanxi*) networks whose growth had been fostered by the Maoist era's economic cellularity, policy vacillations, and waves of political campaigns. To the extent this happened, enterprises were not so much freed from inappropriate controls as they were forced to exchange one kind of entanglement (with distant bureaucratic administrations) for another (with personalistic and perhaps venal local powerholders). They might also find themselves captive to the protectionist policies of authorities in their own area, as, for example, in prohibitions on "exports" of scarce goods needed by other local enterprises or in high demand among consumers; while possibly finding their access to markets outside their region barred by protectionist policies of authorities elsewhere. If the net gain in freedom of enterprises was muted, however, that for the central government's control of the economy was negative. Several years after decentralization began, the central government found itself commanding an ever-diminishing share of total revenues (and embarrassingly unable to collect all the taxes owed it), and exercising ever-diminishing control over use of funds by lower levels of government and by enterprises.

Decentralization, as this suggests, was not tantamount to replacement of planning by market mechanisms. In fact, marketization of the urban economy was pursued only gingerly at the beginning of the 1980s and then temporarily abandoned when the limited introduction of market mechanisms, together with the impact of decentralization, touched off inflation and helped make the state deficit balloon. After the resounding early successes of the rural reforms, however, by late 1984 the reformers considered the time ripe for moving more vigorously toward "market regulation" of the economy.

This meant, first and foremost, price reform. The reformers were determined to reorient the urban economy toward market signals by revising the system of centrally fixed prices. As with agriculture, however, they hesitated to release all prices to find their market level. Instead, the "double-track" price system was adopted in 1985. Under this system, prices of basic inputs supplied to enterprises under the mandatory plan were fixed at a low level, as were the prices of the targeted output. Beyond the targets, however, enterprises were to be free to acquire inputs at market prices, and to sell their output where they wished, at prices they set. The strategy that at least some of the reformers had in mind was that the mandatory-plan, fixed-price targets would be set either to remain unchanged or eventually to decrease. Therefore with economic growth, this portion of economic activity would occupy an ever-decreasing share of every enterprise's output and income, provided, of course, that it was operating efficiently.

The double-track system had different implications for different types of enterprises. Since the planned economy continued to predominate in the heavy industrial sector, the role of market forces was smaller. In the consumer goods sector, the role of market forces was larger, and the profits much higher. But clearly, the role of the market expanded dramatically in the economy as a whole. By 1988, only an estimated 20 or 30 percent of volume of exchange was under state mandatory plans.

Or should we say that the role of something other than the plan expanded? For the dual-track system gave rise to unprecedented inflation and corruption, which undermined attempts to expand the influence of market forces. On the corruption side, local authorities who controlled the supply and allocation of (low) fixed-price goods, as well as enterprises that got access to them, indulged in rounds of selling and reselling these goods at ever higher prices. By 1987 and 1988, to judge from accounts both in the press and by individual Chinese informants, most of the inputs that were supposed to be supplied under the plan were not— while enterprises still had to struggle to produce the planned output to be sold at low fixed prices.

The plan/''market'' transition ran aground in another fashion that helped proliferate the inflationary pressures already created by price reform efforts. With increasing decentralization and growing funds under provincial and local control, localities began investing furiously in the more profitable light and consumer goods industries. The high rates of investment helped to produce the high rates of industrial growth that China has seen under the reforms, but they also pushed up inflation. In part, this is attributable to the runaway expansion of credit (and therefore of money supply) as regional branches of the Bank of China yielded to local authorities' urging. A large part of the explanation since 1985 lies, however, in the gap between the growth rates in light industry and those in basic industries (including energy and transportation) that provided essential inputs. In the two major periods when central controls over credit and investment were most relaxed, in 1980–81 and 1985–87, light industry's growth rates were significantly ahead of heavy industry's, and the gap between industrial growth generally and growth in energy and raw materials supply grew steadily. In 1988 the gap became a chasm: while general industrial production grew by nearly 20 percent, energy and steel production rose by only 4 and 5 percent respectively.

Debates over the proper strategy and pace of price reform continued after the adoption of the dual-track system and intensified as the problems with it grew. In the spring and summer of 1988, remarks by Chinese leaders and the subsequent decisions of a Politburo meeting presaging further dramatic price reforms touched off waves of panic buying. Many bought durable goods as a hedge against inflation. One elderly man spent about half his savings to buy seven refrigerators and 150 kilograms of salt; a report on this case emphasized that he was not speculating in the market, but rather trying to protect his savings against inflation. Multiplied by tens and hundreds of millions, such panic responses so accelerated inflation that economic policy makers back-pedaled and in effect decided to maintain the status quo in the price system.

Attempted reforms in incentives systems did little to reduce the tendencies toward corruption and inflation, while labor incentive reforms went so far off track as to fuel inflation further. The intensification of incentives was aimed at both managers and workers in industrial enterprises. The basic idea behind both managerial and worker incentives was to reorient motivations away from the set of economically passive and risk-averse behaviors that had been fostered under the centrally planned economy, in the direction of entrepreneurial, profit-, and income-maximizing behaviors that would raise economic efficiency and productivity.

For the blue-collar work force, the principal approach was to tie incomes more closely to productivity, and particularly to individual productivity. While the nationwide basic wage scales were retained, new bonuses, piece rates, and various subsidies or in-kind benefits provided at the enterprise level added—or were supposed to add—enormously to the take-home pay of more productive workers. This change certainly widened the real wage differentials between more profitable and less profitable enterprises. However, egalitarian pressures from workers on managers anxious to maintain peace and reliable output meant that within any given enterprise, more often than not bonuses and other benefits were distributed across the board and therefore did not provide the desired incentive. Moreover, worker demands for bonuses and subsidies to offset inflation resulted in a rate of growth in the state-sector wage bill that far outstripped the growth of output. When state regulations limited the amount of cash that could be paid to workers, enterprises expanded in-kind remuneration (e.g., consumer goods) or offered goods and services heavily subsidized by the enterprise.

The incentives reforms most likely to exert an incentive effect were those that threatened the lifelong security of employment that had characterized the state sector for decades. Attempts to eliminate that security across the board met with such resistance that only a diluted "labor contract system," introduced in 1986, could be adopted. The intention was that all new employment in state enterprises would be on terms of contracts for specified periods. Generally these new contract workers would be paid less, and have less job security, than older workers in the same enterprise doing the same work. The system spread slowly; only 8 percent of workers in state enterprises were under contract by 1988.

An experiment in the city of Shenyang was widely publicized in 1988 and must have raised considerable alarm among state-sector workers. The "Shenyang experiment" involved laying off a sizable proportion of the industrial work force, many of them women (paying some limited welfare benefits). With the money saved, remaining workers would receive higher wages for presumably higher productivity. This "worked" in Shenyang—but then, most policy experiments work in China because they receive the expert guidance and supporting resources necessary.

The publicity for the experiment probably raised the anxiety level for many state sector workers. When anxious, Chinese workers are prone to cultivate *guanxi* to minimize their risks, not to raise their productivity.

Contracts of various sorts were also seen as the key to providing more effective incentives for managers. In 1984, experiments began with "factory director responsibility systems," which placed the responsibility for meeting planned targets squarely on the shoulders of the factory manager, thereby presumably shunting the party committee's functions aside into purely political activities. This type of arrangement officially became national policy in 1986. In May 1987, the "contracted management responsibility system," contracting state enterprises out under (supposedly) competitive bidding, was introduced, and by the beginning of 1988, most state-owned firms were persuaded and pressured into adopting some such arrangement. This was to make enterprises more responsible for their own profits (and losses) for a period of three to five years. But in a setting where these firms faced often arbitrarily high prices for their raw materials, had limited freedom to hire and fire, and suffered increasingly the pinch on access to sufficient power supply or transportation facilities, the new "freedoms" accorded them rang hollow. Or, as one authoritative source put it, "Economists said [the contracted management responsibility system] was a compromise which pleased all parties concerned, but which introduced few real changes to industrial management."[4]

Some reformers considered that the competition essential to spur efficiency in state-owned enterprises would only result from challenges from outside the state sector. Such "sectoral incentives" were pursued by permitting, and indeed encouraging, the expansion of collectively and individually owned enterprises. After 1984, the number and output of such enterprises in both rural and urban areas expanded rapidly. Consequently, for the

---

[4]*Asia 1989 Yearbook*, p. 111.

country as a whole, the share of state-owned industry in total industrial output fell from 65 percent in 1985 to 60 percent only two years later. Over the same period, state-owned industry's output rose by 31 percent, while that of collective industry went up by 53 percent, and individually owned industry, by a whopping 180 percent. The work force in collectively and individually owned industries also grew rapidly.

Unfortunately, such developments failed to have the desired impact on state-owned industries. They could call on a variety of strategies. They could use their bureaucratic connections to constrain competition from other enterprises; use contractual relations and control of supplies to place such enterprises in a subordinate role; or rely on their political clout and importance to central and local governmental revenues to obtain subsidies, preferential supplies and credit, and so forth. Indeed, by late 1988, some leading young reform economists argued, in what became a highly controversial set of articles, that only reform of the ownership system of state enterprises would make it possible for price reforms and market incentives to have the desired effect. In the absence of ownership reform, they maintained, ''Our reform is actually endangered by the multiplication and expansion of bureaucratic power in the course of the weakening of administrative power.''[5]

The fourth emphasis in the state sector reforms was on internationalization. The major facets of the internationalization strategy were the expansion of China's international trade and the invitation for foreign capital to invest in China. Behind both such approaches was the eagerness not only to acquire more foreign exchange, but also to acquire more advanced technology, primarily from the West.

Foreign investment grew very slowly at first, and as it grew it was concentrated in only a few areas. Foreign capital was attracted through two principal avenues. The first was the construc-

---

[5] Hua, Zhang, and Luo, "Ten Years of Reform."

tion of "special economic zones" (SEZs) where it was hoped that foreign capital, released from many of the controls present in the rest of China, would rapidly construct industrial bases largely oriented toward export markets. Foreign capital did pour into the SEZs, but so did bureaucratic graft and corruption. By 1988 it was still not clear just how much of a net gain the SEZs represented; much of their output was diverted for domestic sales, while much of their input had to be imported, and many of the profits seemed to have been siphoned off by dishonest officials and managers. Foreign businesses grew increasingly wary of invitations to make further investments.

Foreign capital remained initially skittish about the other avenue offered for investment, that of engaging in joint ventures outside the SEZs. Much of the reluctance stemmed from the lack of clear legal protection, as the Chinese regulations on joint ventures and on taxation of foreign enterprises took years to appear. Meanwhile, bureaucratic snarls, lack of foreign-exchange access for essential inputs, uncertainty over state price policy, shortages of energy and water, and constraints on freedom to hire and fire as well as controls over wage rates all made foreign businesses slow to invest. Foreign investment only really began to take off in 1986, building momentum up to 1988, when U.S. $2.6 billion was invested, and new contracts totaling over U.S. $5 billion were signed. Hong Kong capital accounted for about 40 percent of the total foreign investments, and coastal areas, particularly Guangdong, received the lion's share of the foreign capital input.

Foreign trade expanded much earlier in the reform era. Barring a couple of plateaus caused by state readjustment policies, both imports and exports zoomed upward steadily after 1978, ending the economic autarchy that was a Maoist article of faith. By 1988 foreign trade accounted for approximately 10 percent of the national income, much higher in the booming coastal provinces. Many state-owned trading companies were established or expanded below the central level. They were allowed to organize complicated export-production contracts that linked foreign buyers, state-owned enterprises, rural factories, and foreign suppliers of inputs and machinery. While only a limited number of enterprises were given the right to import on their own authority, the retention of significant portions of foreign exchange by local enterprises and governments meant that many import decisions (and short-term borrowing of foreign funds) were made outside of central state control.

For all the difficulties encountered by urban state-sector reforms, there were undeniably enormous improvements in both production and standards of living. The real rate of industrial growth for 1980–87 was well over 10 percent per annum. This, together with the rapid agricultural growth rate, gave China the world's third fastest growing economy during that period. The fruits of industrial growth could be seen in the profusion of the urban landscape. Motorcycles and then automobiles and trucks under private ownership appeared in growing numbers. High-rise apartment buildings spread through the cities and into the surrounding fields. By 1987, the average urban resident's real income had doubled compared with 1978, and living space had increased by some 60 percent. The durable consumer goods possessed by urban households proliferated: by 1987, every 100 households gloried in 177 bicycles, 145 sofas, 104 electric fans, 67 washing machines, 65 black-and-white televisions, 35 color televisions, 57 tape recorders, and 20 electric refrigerators. Young men in the larger cities wore leather jackets and jeans; many young women could be seen in high-heeled red boots, leather slacks, and makeup. The only form of consumption that appears to have fallen is that of grains and vegetables—to be replaced by higher consumption of meat and fish, confections, and alcohol.

As with the rural areas, however, there was a darker side to the picture. If private employment and opportunities to make money quickly on the market grew, so too did illegal currency dealings, drug trade, prostitution, and violent crime. Corruption and graft, despite intermittent crackdowns, seem to have become a way of life for any of those in the public sector who could work out a scam. Three billion dollars of foreign exchange currency leaked out of the country in 1988, probably a sign of large-scale corruption tied to capital flight. Billions more in Chinese currency were raked off by enterprise managers and government and party officials. A massive scandal involving high-ranking officials rocked Hainan in 1986.

Regional disparities widened dramatically, as they did for the rural sector, with the coastal provinces pulling rapidly ahead of the interior provinces.[6] National meetings of provincial-level party and state officials were characterized by often bitter complaints from leaders of interior provinces.

From Reform to Crisis

The reform decade brought unprecedented growth to the Chinese economy, probably far surpassing what any of the reform leaders had initially dared to hope for. The growth figures compare quite favorably with those of other countries in the developing world; indeed, they nearly match the performance of South Korea during its period of take-off from the mid-1960s to the mid-1970s. Development, then, would seem to be on its way.

Any process of economic development is going to be uneven. Some people and places will pull ahead, while others fall, relatively, behind. Some sectors wither while others burgeon. Great economic improvements will entail some social costs. Efficiency will, in some ways, undercut equity. Quantitative growth over a certain period of time builds up structural tensions that require structural change with, perhaps, a short period of quantitative

---

[6] Central state taxation policy played a role here. The shift to lump-sum payments from provinces to Beijing introduced after 1984 left increasing amounts of funds in the hands of provincial and local authorities and enterprises in the faster-growing coastal areas, which meant further acceleration of their growth as they reinvested. The poorer interior provinces started out poor and, with few funds of their own to invest, faced a future of falling ever further behind.

stagnation while the necessary adjustments are made. Growing economies experience growing pains. This does not, however, ensure that every painful economic situation is just "growing pains."

By 1988, China's economic situation was painful indeed, and matters came to a head by the fall. Two meetings of central leaders (the Politburo at Beidaihe in August and the Third Plenum of the Thirteenth Central Committee in September) thrashed over the mounting problems that existing reform proposals seemed powerless to affect (except for the worse).

Central government tax revenues had essentially stagnated since 1985; deficits had been disguised by accounting methods that included foreign and domestic borrowing as "revenues." If those were subtracted, the state budgetary deficit for 1987 was not eight billion yuan but thirty-five billion! By mid-1988, China's foreign debt, almost nonexistent four years earlier, was forty billion U.S. dollars. Imports increasingly outstripped exports, and although the country had good exchange reserves, they could not be maintained indefinitely with a mounting balance-of-trade deficit and with foreign loans falling due.

The demands on the state exchequer, meanwhile, were growing. While the state fended off pleas for increased state investment, from provincial and local leaders as well as from central ministries, certain investments remained essential, particularly in transportation and energy.

The challenge of ensuring urban food supplies loomed as an increasingly expensive one. Faced with difficulties in getting farmers to grow and deliver grain, national policy makers felt it necessary to raise purchasing prices, while trying to hold the line on retail prices of grain in the cities. Subsidies for grain and edible oils alone rose from six to seven billion yuan in 1978 to twenty-two billion yuan in 1988 and were expected to hit thirty-one billion yuan in 1989. In 1988, total central state subsidies to enterprises and for retail prices amounted to about one-third of total state budgetary expenditures.

What lent the tone of urgency to the central leaders' deliberations, however, was the problem of inflation. Inflation took off in 1988, reaching an annual rate of about 19 percent in the first half of the year. Despite government declarations of intention to tighten credit and cut back on excessive investment spending, the rate continued to climb. The official rate for inflation from December 1987 to December 1988 was 27 percent; the real rate was undoubtedly much higher. China's official statistical agency reported that surveys indicated a drop in real incomes for over a third of urban households in 1988. As anyone with Chinese friends well knows, many above the bottom third felt threatened by inflation; many staved off that threat only by exhausting themselves moonlighting; and young people felt they faced a dead-end future of low pay and boring work—if they could find a job at all.

The blame for inflation was not assigned, however, to the state budget deficit, but to a number of other factors, all of which had certainly contributed to it. The domestic credit system was seriously overheated. "Extrabudgetary" expenditures and borrowing by enterprises and agencies had grossly inflated demand for producer and consumer goods. The money in circulation had expanded much faster than output. (While labor productivity rose an estimated 115 percent from 1978 to 1986, "purchasing power" rose by 285 percent.) Price-reform proposals in an inflationary climate had exacerbated the inflation.

The solution adopted was essentially to put reforms on hold. As noted above, price reform was postponed indefinitely. Priority went to reasserting central control over allocations of materials and to a two-year austerity program aimed at severely cutting back on the forces overheating the economy: particularly investment and credit. Subsidies, on the other hand, which from an economic perspective only encourage overconsumption and thus inflate demand signals to producers, were left largely untouched, or when cut were resumed under other guises. While the austerity program to some extent contracted credit, employment, and incomes, however, decentralization had left enough resources and alternative channels in the hands of local authorities, who had their own good reasons for encouraging overinvestment, so that the inflation was not brought under control.

The Double Dilemma

Certainly, these are all problems—but where, one may ask, is the dilemma? From a strictly economic perspective, the solution of China's current developmental impasse requires the austerity measures described above, probably with the addition of thoroughgoing price reform and an elimination of most state subsidies. Economically speaking, China has no other choice if it is to meet its growth and development goals. Adjustments in the economic system and structures, the elimination of entitlements, the marginalization of some producers, and the bankrupting of inefficient enterprises may be painful but are essential adjustments for the long-run health of the economy, and thus, for the success of the reforms.

Yet this is a limited perspective, excluding some of the factors central to resolving the problems that Chinese reform now faces. The key question is not "What economic policies will solve the current economic problems?" but "Why do the economic measures adopted get either lost or distorted in the course of implementation?" It is here that the reform process has foundered, not so much on contradictions in economic policy (which do indeed exist) as on the political economy of the People's Republic, which continues to require the pursuit of contradictory goals, while making it increasingly impossible to realize them.

It is tempting to cast the problem simply (if this complexity could be called simple!) in terms of the dilemma of socialist reform: that of making the transition from a centrally planned command economy to a mixed-ownership economy responding to market signals. There is a rich literature on this dilemma, based mostly on Eastern European reform experience, and some of the scholarship on China has drawn upon that tradition. Ignoring the varieties of interpretation for brevity's sake, let me merely note the central propositions in this line of analysis.[7]

The first such proposition is that socialist systems making the plan-to-market transition tend to get stuck midway between the two, frequently getting not the best but the worst of both worlds. The second proposition is that one major reason for the stickiness of this transition is the persistent "resource hunger" and "excess demand" that characterize the command economy's economics of shortage, and that describe the typical behavior of economic managers in such a system. In effect, the incentive signals coming from the planned economy continue to interfere with the incentive effect of signals from the market. The third proposition is that economic managers' responses to market signals are more likely to be bureaucratic bargaining and political lobbying (or bribery) for exceptions, subsidies, and special treatment from the state than to be market-entrepreneurial adjustments. The fourth proposition is that smaller and non-state-owned producers are more likely to have to make market-entrepreneurial adjustments than are larger, state-owned producers with more political clout. As just one example of how such political clout might arise, apart from personal contacts and parallel bureaucratic mentality, consider the Chinese tobacco industry, the monopoly over which is held by the state-owned China Tobacco Corporation. In 1987, this single state corporation delivered seventeen billion yuan in

---

[7]Janos Kornai's work has been of the greatest influence in developing my sense of these propositions. See, for example, *Contradictions and Dilemmas: Studies on the Socialist Economy and Society* (Cambridge: The MIT Press, 1986); and "The Hungarian Reform Process: Visions, Hopes, and Reality," in *Remaking the Economic Institutions of Socialism: China and Eastern Europe*, ed. Victor Nee and David Stark (Stanford: Stanford University Press, 1989), pp. 32–94; and J. Kornai and Zs. Daniel, "The Chinese Economic Reform—As Seen by Hungarian Economists," *Acta Oeconomica* 36, 3–4 (1986): 289–305. See also the extremely informative and sophisticated discussion by Stark and Nee, "Toward an Institutional Analysis of State Socialism," in *Remaking the Economic Institutions*, ed. Nee and Stark, pp. 1–31.

taxes and profit to the state treasury—over 7 percent of total budgetary revenues. Because smaller producers must use inputs from and sell output to the larger firms, however, the "market signals" they encounter will be distorted by the preferences accorded the larger enterprises by the central plan. For China, we should advance a more socially specific proposition as well: state-socialist development during the entire era from 1949 to the late 1970s created and fostered the institutional entrenchment of social groups and social interests connected with central planning and state enterprises—not just bureaucrats and managers, but state-sector workers as well. Efforts at economic reform outside this sector may receive considerable support from these influential groups insofar as those reforms increase the resources available to the state sector, as raw materials, revenues, or consumption goods. Economic reforms that are immediately costly either directly or indirectly to these groups will be opposed with all the considerable political resources at their command, even though the eventual result of such reforms might be to increase the net resources in the state sector.

Where a reform coalition is able to push through such reform policies despite resistance, the affected groups will lobby for, and get, a variety of specific exceptions of special treatment, roughly in proportion to their relative power in the state system. The result is a snowballing scramble for patched-together "deals" at all levels, turning the reform edifice into a jerry-built structure, distorting market signals, and inflating inefficiencies beyond those of the previous centrally controlled system. One point should be underlined here: the fact that increasing numbers of enterprises and individuals operate outside the plan does not mean that they operate within the market. While "escapes" from direct bureaucratic controls may be attractive strategies for individuals and groups, they are still trapped within the distorted environment created by state-sector actors' strategic responses, and the cumulative effect of the actions of all may be further to exacerbate those distortions. Therefore, while figures on numbers of nonstate workers, output of nonstate enterprises, and volumes traded outside the state commercial system may indicate erosion of state monopoly controls, they do not provide a reliable gauge of the effectiveness (in any meaningful sense) of reform.

Measures that further relax central controls or release prices, in this environment, merely expand the opportunities—and incentives—for bureaucratic deals, speculation, and corruption and exacerbate the distortionary forces. Faced with the economic consequences of these dynamics, many economic policy makers will see no alternative but to reimpose central controls and pull back on market reforms. For the time being, these have won in China.

But why did they win, and why was their win so long in doubt, and achieved only at the cost of bloodshed? To answer such questions, we must look beyond the dilemma of socialist reform, to a second dilemma now confronting the Chinese developmental process: that of linking economic development strategy with state authority and legitimacy. If the first dilemma illuminates China's similarities with some East European systems, the second underlines its parallels with much of the Third World under capitalism. Such parallels have grown increasingly apparent during the reform era. Certainly this is true of the economic and social consequences of the rapid but unbalanced growth of the past ten years in China, which matches the growth, for example, of Brazil and Mexico in the 1960s and 1970s. The genius of the Chinese reform program, it would seem, is that it has managed to compress into just one decade the achievements that took Latin American countries several decades to accomplish: massive rural-urban migration, marginalization of large segments of the peasantry and of the agricultural economy, open unemployment, urban crime and indigence, growing international debt and dependence, runaway inflation, corruption of public officials and institutions, and finally, political instability.

Of course, political life was unstable during the Cultural Revolution decade, as the post-Mao leadership never tired of repeating. The legitimacy of the socialist system and of the party leading it was not fundamentally threatened, however, even when most party leaders themselves came under attack. I would suggest that this was so because the party delivered on certain key promises that underlay its implicit social contract with the Chinese population, concluded in 1949: basic security of subsistence (afforded through basic ration allocations in rural communes, and the subsidized retail food network in the cities), guaranteed employment, and—for cities in general and for many rural areas—gradually rising standards of living.[8]

Moreover, the strategy of development pursued during the three decades after 1949 strengthened the party's grip on power by creating certain groups whose status, welfare, and very existence rested on their roles within the politico-economic system. These client groups, especially urban bureaucrats and rural cadres above production-team level, exercised local power in the name of the party and received in return an extra share of social status, economic reward, and mobility opportunities. Urban workers as a whole may be regarded as another client group, enlarged tremendously in the course of industrialization, with living standards (including access to health and welfare benefits) and educational opportunities well above those of the peasantry, and with far easier conditions of work and far greater security of income.

If the economic stagnation of the late Maoist era, coupled with popular disenchantment with repeated political campaigns, substantially eroded the party's popularity, the party could nonetheless still count on a strong residual legitimacy among the population as a whole, and on considerable influence over the principal client groups in particular. The early phase of the reform process, by putting land and much more income into the hands of the peasants, and much more food on

---

[8] That the standard of living rose quite slowly is not of great importance, since lack of contact with the outside world and minimization of disparities in domestic incomes meant that expectations of improvements remained quite modest.

everyone's table, seemed to promise only greater legitimacy.

How, then, from its high point in 1984, could the party's legitimacy, authority, and prestige have fallen so far and so fast? Here, I would argue, the problem predates 1984, although it has been exacerbated since then. The implicit economic strategy underlying the reforms has begun transforming China into a much more typical Third World setting. Despite the avid interest in the Asian "little dragons" evinced by many reform economists and policy makers, the basic development strategy used during the reform era most closely matches those that have been employed in large parts of Latin America, featuring a sectoral emphasis on industrialization, especially heavy industrialization, and a rural development approach emphasizing concentration of resources among highly commercialized, larger-scale, and highly capitalized farmers, often oriented toward exports.[9]

The country's progress in applying such a strategy has so transformed the social landscape as to undermine the basis of the party's old social contract with the populace, and threaten the social and economic survival of the old client groups.

The old social contract—particularly its subsistence and security guarantees—has been undermined in myriad ways. Most prominent, however, are the loss of basic food guarantees with the elimination of rural collective distributions, the loss of employment guarantees in both rural and urban areas, and the inflationary spiral that threatens the perceived future security of urban residents. It is interesting to note in this context that the rural policies, by fostering the rise of a new rich peasant class, and more recently by promoting concentration of landholdings, have undermined the relatively equal rural social structure that some analysts have argued underlay the successful industrialization of the "little dragons" and their relative political stability.

---

[9]See Bruce F. Johnston and William C. Clark, *Redesigning Rural Development: A Strategic Perspective* (Baltimore: Johns Hopkins University Press, 1982); and Merilee Grindle, *State and Countryside: Development Policy and Agrarian Politics in Latin America* (Baltimore: Johns Hopkins University Press, 1986).

The threat to the old client groups has stemmed from the erosion of the powers of rural cadres and the competition from new rural entrepreneurs, from the attempted removal of urban party bureaucrats from economic management, from the emphasis placed on increased reliance on technical expertise, and from the rise of a new class of wealthy entrepreneurs in the cities.

In this context, the party could pursue two different political strategies: the first, to offer compensatory benefits to the general populace and/or the old client groups; the second, to cultivate new client groups. In practice it has attempted to do both. And by so doing, it has ensnared itself in a vicious spiral of attempts to undo with one hand what it has just done with another—a spiral increasingly difficult to break through without bringing down the whole political edifice.

A handful of examples will suffice. Take, for instance, the whole food-price dilemma. Here the party-state retained its commitment to maintaining a cheap basic food supply for the cities, while aiming to provide more food than before. So producer prices had to rise, but subsidies rose with them, reducing the resources available in the state budget for productive or infrastructure investment. When prices of nonbasic foods were allowed to float closer to market levels, compensatory payments were to be made to urban workers' wages and sometimes to urban residents at large. Every announcement of price reform brought with it assurances that prices would not really rise, or not that much, coupled with further subsidies and therefore further inflation. Meanwhile, food production became more expensive and less attractive to farmers, and ensuring production and sales deliveries entailed either increasing favoritism toward larger farmers or increasingly coercive measures toward ordinary farmers.

Or consider the urban factory wage and employment reforms. Factory managers' ability to move effectively in the market and turn a profit might depend vitally on the freedom to hire and fire, but workers hired under the old lifelong employment system could not be subjected to such changes without causing considerable disaffection. Therefore, only new workers would be hired under the new contractual employment arrangements, and any gains to efficiency would be only very gradually accomplished. Meanwhile, the contract workers would have to be squeezed more to make up for the inefficiency of and generous benefits accorded to the "lifers."

Cultivation of new clients was no simpler. Take, for example, Deng Xiaoping's attempts to revivify the party itself. He had hoped to achieve "renewal" through a thoroughgoing but bureaucratically conducted purge at all levels, then by recruiting more intellectuals and people with technical skills into the party and making contributions to modernization a major criterion for advancement within the party ranks. What happened, however, was that older and less qualified functionaries blocked not only the promotion but also the use of the skills of the younger and better educated coworkers. Thus, older cadres were resentful and disaffected, while younger ones were disillusioned and disaffected. With morale low, and the old "moral" criteria for leadership in abeyance, abuse of the "back door" to privileges and perquisites escalated, and corruption cases mushroomed far beyond the capacity—or will—of the party or state to deal with them.

With its amalgam of the dilemmas of socialist reform and politico-economic strategy, China developed a particularly pernicious syndrome during the reform era, as policy makers attempted to retain the old bases of legitimacy and authority in an environment that could no longer accommodate them without enormous economic and political cost, and often not even then. In theory, it is not utterly impossible to resolve those dilemmas. They might, perhaps, be addressed more effectively through an application of what economic advisers are wont to call "political will." To some extent, that is what the theorists of the "new authoritarianism" were calling for in late 1988 and early 1989, insofar as they saw themselves formulating some political solution to the economic impasse of the reforms.

Leaving aside the question of whether these theorists understood the dynamics of the phenomenon they were talking about (there is strong evidence that they did not), the problem of invoking this particular form of political solution is that it matters very much who invokes it. The quandary that authoritarian solutions are supposed to address is that painful choices have to be made to promote economic development, and all social groups are too wedded to their own particularistic interests to permit the necessary political decisions, through open politics, to be made and acted upon. But every development strategy and every sociopolitical structure implies a particular hierarchy of pain. From the development-strategy perspective, certain sectors and groups must pay disproportionately. And from the perspective of those at the top of the sociopolitical structure, certain sectors and groups (themselves, first and foremost) will not be made to pay, and indeed will enjoy disproportionate benefits.

The hierarchy of pain and profit grew steeper in the course of the reforms, through both legitimate and illegitimate means. If the Chinese leadership's unity increasingly fragmented in the course of such change, it is no wonder. Even if most of them are willing to countenance the growth of a bourgeoisie of sorts outside the party, and some growth of "bourgeoisie inside the party" so decried by the Maoists, many of them must have realized that a corrupt, venal, hidebound, and inefficient bourgeoisie does nobody any good and the party itself a great deal of harm. And those among them who were corrupt, venal, hidebound, and inefficient, whether bourgeois or not, had more and more to lose. No one, meanwhile, possessed a credible economic formula for resolving the differences over reform policy, because no such formula is possible in a polity that is out of step with both economy and society.

The post-Mao leadership had staked their legitimacy on economic performance, and they were caught in an impasse of their own construction. Tragedy was perhaps not inevitable, but significant instability, hardship, and social upheaval certainly were. At the moment, the chosen solution is for coercion. Deng Xiaoping is reported to be enamored of seeking truth from facts. In the spring of 1989, facing facts—about a million of them gathered right under his nose in Tiananmen Square—he tried to bludgeon the facts away. Yet the octogenarian hardliners know from their own experiences as organizers of revolutionary forces that coercion can silence opposition but is powerless to elicit productive cooperation. Coercion cannot resolve the underlying dilemmas; these remain and may prove more intractable now than before. Although the political conflict has recently held center stage, it is the underlying crisis in the political economy that accounts for the massive popular support for the student movement and for the disarray among the party leadership. It is those same issues that seem already to render hollow the victory of those who have ''won'' the recent rounds in the struggle.

Four

LEARNING HOW TO PROTEST

Frank Niming

> Call: Citizens of Beijing, come to action and participate in the
> world-wide demonstration of the 28th. Tomorrow at around 10
> o'clock we will depart. Itinerary: All troops will get together and
> wait for orders at Jianguomen.
>
> —Pamphlet from Beijing University

THE PEOPLE'S MOVEMENT as it unfolded during the spring of
1989 was not the straightforward confrontation, as it would seem
at first sight, between the forces of Good and Evil, between an
oppressed people and its wicked government. Rather, it was what
I would like to call a "total event," a sequence of actions expressing all of the fundamental problems and conflicts of interest
within a society, and forcing all groups into the political arena.
Because of its complexity and denseness it will be impossible for
a long time to gauge its exact meaning and impact on Chinese
history. What is certain, however, is that Chinese society and
politics will never be the same again. The People's Movement
was a turning point in Chinese history. It forged new alliances,
deepened and even created oppositions, and shaped new (or rein-
vented and reshaped old) modes and symbols of political action.

This chapter will focus on one aspect of the movement, the
demonstrations of students, journalists, intellectuals, and finally
"the masses," mainly using my own interviews and observations
in Beijing between April 18 and June 4, 1989. I will analyze the
movement as it unfolded in the streets as an interactional learning

process. I will try to show how different groups learned how to demonstrate in different ways and at different times in response to the actions (demonstrations, statements, violence, hunger strike) of other actors (individuals, factions, groups).

The key actors in this process were the student activists. Drawing on the experience of earlier (1980, 1986, 1988) student activism, they knew they were facing two crucial strategic problems. The first was how to avoid an immediate government crackdown. This had two aspects. First, they should show themselves to be independent from the day-to-day factional struggle within the CCP. If not, another faction might perceive the students as an immediate threat and use its power to crush the student movement before its political opponents had time to use the students to their own political advantage. The way Deng Xiaoping had used the 1978–79 Democracy Wall Movement had already shown the intraparty political clout of such movements for those who know how to use them. Second, the students had to avoid criticizing the political system as such, otherwise the party as a whole might unite against them, label their movement counter-revolutionary, and crush it before it could gather political momentum. In sum, the students had to make use of divisions within the party leadership without getting embroiled in them.

The second strategic problem facing the students was how to mobilize the mass of the urban population for their cause. The students knew they would be ploughing fertile soil thanks to the mounting dissatisfaction about the results of the urban reforms (corruption, inflation, decreased job security, growing income inequality). Moreover, at least since the May Fourth Movement of 1919, students have played a much more prominent political role in China than in the West. Chinese students can fall back on a tradition of protest in which they repeatedly have played the role of the conscience of the nation, speaking out on behalf of the oppressed mass of the people. The students also knew, however, that it was extremely difficult for the people to side openly and demonstrate together with them.

There are several reasons why the average Chinese was extremely hesitant to take to the streets. First among these is the understandable fear of later repercussions. Demonstrating in China is more than just a regular form of political action. In the eyes of the authorities it constitutes a direct challenge to the system and the leadership of the party itself. It is potentially counterrevolutionary behavior that falls outside of the realms of legitimate expression of dissent. Demonstrating means that one risks most, if not everything, of what one is and has.

The second reason why the Beijing citizens found it difficult to join the students in their protests has to do with the nature of political control in Chinese society. Although China does have specialized control agencies, their work is limited to the more special cases. (The Ministry of Public Security, however, apparently does have known agents in every work unit.) Unlike the Soviet Union, where the KGB uses a high profile as a deterrent, political control is enmeshed with the bureaucratically organized political structure itself. With the family the work unit (*gongzuo danwei*, or simply *danwei*) is the most important social unit for each individual. Here are kept the personal files (*dang'an*) of all members of the unit, in which everything of more than passing interest, public or private, is recorded. What one does or says in the work unit will more often than not be reported to the leadership of the unit, who can then decide to include it in one's file. Once entered, such information can be dug up any time. This is all the more threatening because so many things (housing, social security, medical care, income, social status) are dependent on the work unit. Because of this, one's personal interests are intimately bound up with the unit, thus giving its leadership great leverage over the members.

As so much is dependent on the unit, it is the primary reference group for all working individuals. Since its victory in 1949, the party has been at great pains to prevent other organizations from emerging that are not directly or indirectly subordinate to its own bureaucratic supervision. It has concentrated most social and political functions in the work units and not in the hands of specialized agencies. Therefore, it seemed only natural to my interview informants that if they demonstrated they would do so with their work units. In urban China there does not yet exist an alternative organizational focus beyond the work unit where social activities, including demonstrations, can be set up. This gives the party and the state a sturdy grip over the life of its citizens. In normal times, demonstrations or other forms of political action would need the permission, or at least tacit approval, of the unit leader. That demonstrations did eventually take place during the later stages of the movement was a major breakthrough. This breakthrough was only made possible because of very special circumstances (the political deadlock within the leadership, the mounting dissatisfaction among the people), the level of political sophistication of the students, and a learning process that took place during the movement itself. Initially, however, the students could not hope for the active support of the people. During the initial stages the challenge was to create avenues for the people to express their sympathy without getting tainted politically. The death of the former party general secretary, Hu Yaobang, on April 15 provided the students with a politically sufficiently neutral occasion to start the ball rolling.

Phase One: The First Demonstrations at the Square

After dinner on the evening of April 18, I went for a walk down Chang'an Avenue. Arriving at Tiananmen Square, I noticed several thousand mainly young people around the Monument to the People's Heroes. Some were carrying wreaths of paper flowers. In that morning's *People's Daily*, I had read that professors at Beijing University had placed similar wreaths at the monument the previous day to mourn the death of Hu Yaobang. I had assumed, however, that this was carefully organized and orchestrated by the government. Yet events proved to be quite different. It was strikingly similar to the attempts to mourn Zhou Enlai in

1976, which led to the famous Tiananmen Incident of April 5. By contrast, in 1989, the atmosphere was relaxed, almost joyful, and completely different from what I remembered from descriptions of the 1976 events. To give an impression of the general mood that evening, here are some passages from my field notes, which I wrote immediately after returning home.

> Most of the people [around the monument] are curious bystanders like myself, but several youths are busily copying down each others poems [pasted on the sides of the monument]. Facing the Great Hall of the People there is more activity. . . . Focus of attention is a group of about 300 youths sitting on the pavement. Every now and then one of them gets up to say something completely incomprehensible followed by loud cheers of agreement by the others. . . . All in all the atmosphere is more like a game of soccer during a warm summer evening than of excited political action. People are using it as an opportunity for a family outing together with wife and child, and the number of well-dressed young couples, usually concentrated in the public parks around this time of day, is high.

It transpired that these youths sitting on the ground were students from Beijing and People's universities. They were discussing a set of demands[1] to be submitted to the representatives who were meeting in the Great Hall of the People. After drafting their demands and sending a delegation into the hall to submit them to the leaders, the students began a demonstration, carrying around the square a paper wreath and a banner with the words "Democratic Spirit" (*minzhu hun*) in honor of Hu Yaobang, eventually placing them on the monument. In this relatively modest way a

---

[1]These demands, as related to me by one of the students, were: clarification of the reasons for Hu Yaobang's resignation as party general secretary in 1987 and about the people behind this; clarification of the reasons for and background to the "anti–bourgeois liberalization campaign" that followed Hu's resignation; publication of high cadres' incomes; repeal of the regulations restricting students' off-campus political activities; legalization of nonofficial (*minban*) publications; that representatives meeting in the hall come outside to discuss the demands with the students; that the *People's Daily* run a factual account of what was happening there that evening.

movement started that eventually would mobilize almost the entire population of Beijing and pose a direct threat to the survival of China's political leaders. Nevertheless, almost all elements that would later come to the fore more clearly as the movement developed were already present.

First, active demonstrators and passive bystanders were separated from each other, albeit not as clearly as during later demonstrations. The role of the bystanders was important, however, because their numbers add political weight to the students' activities.

Second, many of the original demands would resurface repeatedly, becoming progressively less moderate and sharper. For example, the demands to clarify who was responsible for Hu's resignation and the anti–bourgeois liberalization campaign can be read as the direct precursors of the later demand for the resignation (*cizhi*), and still later the downfall (*dadao*), of Deng Xiaoping, Li Peng, and Yang Shangkun.

Third, democracy, nationalism, and loyalty to the CCP were linked directly together. According to the students, there was no contradiction between democracy and socialism. On the contrary, the demand was only for a speedup of the democratization process as part of the official reform of the political system.

Fourth, reporting by foreign journalists was essential to the students. It allowed them to spread their message to the broadest possible audience both inside and outside China without state censorship. Moreover, foreign reporting made it appreciably more difficult for the authorities simply to ignore the movement and also raised the diplomatic price of possible repression.

Phase Two: Bystanders' Support

After this first demonstration, which I witnessed, the movement developed quickly. Mourning Hu Yaobang proved to be an effective way to navigate around the rocks of swift government suppression. It allowed the students to avoid identification with the faction of pragmatic reformers led by General Secretary Zhao Ziyang, while at the same time being politically neutral enough to forestall immediate repression by a leadership closing ranks in the face of a common threat. Nevertheless, most of the more conservative leaders, including Deng Xiaoping, were seriously disturbed, as was made clear by the April 26 editorial in the *People's Daily* condemning the student movement as a conspiracy. Interestingly enough, it was precisely this editorial (testimony to their successful solution to the first strategic problem) that helped the students solve the second: how to forge a link between their movement and the dissatisfied mass of Beijing people.

During the first demonstrations at the Square, the people did not dare join the students in their protest. Many were sympathetic to their demands, but knew all too well what the price of participation could be. Beijing's citizens simply did not think that the student movement of late April was the appropriate occasion for such a drastic step. Most thought that the authorities would quickly put an end to the student protests, leaving those who had supported them open to the authorities' wrath. In a sense, this was a self-fulfilling prophecy. Since everybody thought that the students alone were too weak and too isolated, they remained too weak and isolated to alarm the authorities.

On April 27, the students organized a demonstration protesting the previous day's *People's Daily* editorial. I was out of town, but I have compiled the following account from a detailed report in *Xin guancha* (New observer) and later discussions with friends and interviewees. This demonstration was much larger than those previously, and bystanders along its route expressed their support for the students for the first time. People gave money, popsicles, food, and drinks to the students. This added new elements to the symbolic repertoire of the movement, which would resurface again during the period of the hunger strike and the occupation of the Square. It also solved an important strategic problem. The people's open support for the students on this occasion was related to the government's reaction to the demonstrations. The students were merely demanding a dialogue with the leaders to discuss the pressing problems facing China. In their editorial, and earlier through the violence used against student demonstrators at Xinhua Gate in the early morning of April 20, government and party leaders made clear that they did not intend to talk to the students. This gave the impression that the leaders were indifferent to the problems of ordinary people. As a result, the students garnered more support than they had received hitherto.

As the people could not demonstrate themselves, the students had to continue to play this active role for them. The student demonstrations represented the silent frustrations of the population. For this reason, the students continued using relatively empty concepts like "democracy" and "science," which were never given any specific content, together with concrete demands such as "down with official speculation" (*dadao guandao*), on which everybody could agree. Since these demands had little to do with the specific interests and frustrations of individual segments of the population, everybody could identify with the movement. Each individual, as an anonymous member of "the people," could give the students the mandate to represent his or her specific, but during the demonstrations unstated, frustrations about the system, the leadership, and its policies. For example, when I asked a bicycle repairman whether his business had already been contracted out to him, he volunteered the following opinion:

> My business has been contracted out (*chengbao*) to me for a while now, or actually it has been only partially contracted out. Now, I am taking the financial risks, but the decisions are still made by the cadres of the organization to which my business belongs. They aren't doing a thing, but nevertheless hang on to their positions, and that is the reason the people are demonstrating now.

At the end of April, the students and the people, in reaction to the inflexibility and arrogance of the leadership, developed a form of political action in which the students acted as the representatives of the people.[2] The anonymity and outward passivity of the bystander role gave the people a way to circumvent the system of political control in China, which focuses on them as members of work units and not as citizens. During the demonstrations, the mandate of the people was expressed and renewed again and again. The slogans shouted and written on banners, and the petitions signed and presented to the leaders were in a sense less important. The essential political facts were that a demonstration took place and that the people expressed their support for the demonstrators.

Phase Three: Bicycle Demonstrations and Journalists

Large-scale demonstrations supported by the people as a newly discovered political weapon gave the student movement the impetus it needed to carry on beyond the symbolic date of May 4, the seventieth anniversary of the 1919 May Fourth Movement. With the passing of May 4, the students were faced with the same problems as before the April 27 demonstration. Which is the next symbolic date to work toward? In what way can we keep the movement alive and the initiative in our own hands? The students found a temporary solution in the bicycle demonstrations of May 9 and 10, while the arrival in Beijing of Mikhail Gorbachev on May 15 became the new target date. At the same time, the independent demonstrations of journalists gave the movement a new dimension. During the May 4 demonstration, journalists from several prominent newspapers in

---

[2] There were two reasons that the students could and dared demonstrate while ordinary people were immobilized by their own fear and the strength of political control. First, students have a long tradition of protest on behalf of the whole nation. They have built up a sense of mission, the feeling that the future of the nation depends on them. Second, under pressure from wave after wave of student protests in the 1980s, the political control system on the campuses had gradually given way to a whole network of independent student clubs. The students had built up the organizational basis and leadership structures needed for swift political action, the general absence of which had made it impossible for ordinary people to demonstrate.

Beijing had organized their own demonstration, which had joined up with the students. At that time, however, their demonstration and demands provided a mere footnote to the student demonstration, and neither I nor my informants noticed the activities of the journalists.

Students and journalists were quick to link up and coordinate their activities. For the first and last time, a group seized the opportunity created by the student movement to organize their own demonstrations to push their own demands: freedom of the press. Passive sympathizers had become active participants. Of crucial importance was that many of the journalists were also prominent intellectuals. The new and open alliance between journalists and students constituted an important precedent. It set the example for the later, wider support of intellectuals for the student hunger strikers, which proved to be of crucial significance.

The immediate issue around which the journalists rallied was the closure in April of the liberal and semi-independent Shanghai newspaper *World Economic Herald* (*Shijie jingji daobao*), ostensibly because of its calls for a thorough reevaluation of Hu Yaobang's role as well as the students' demands. The journalists sought to use this action to express their dissatisfaction about the severe limitations imposed on their own reporting of the movement, and about the whole issue of press freedom in general. Freedom of the press had been one of the seven original demands of the students. When the journalists organized demonstrations and submitted a petition to the leadership on May 9 and 10, they became the focus of attention, with the students temporarily receding to a supporting role. During the students' own bicycle demonstrations, a new way of demonstrating chosen because it allowed for coverage of much larger distances,[3] the students demanded press freedom and ridiculed the lack of independence of the newspapers with slogans like "The *People's Daily*: Bull-

---

[3] The bicycle demonstrations were quickly abandoned because they were very difficult to contain and severely affected the strong sense of orderliness and organization that was one of the students' most powerful weapons against government propaganda accusing them of creating disorder.

shit!'' (*Renmin ribao: Hu shuo ba dao*). Suitably, these demonstrations no longer had Tiananmen Square as their symbolic destination, but the compound of the *People's Daily* in the eastern suburbs.

Phase Four: Support for the Hunger Strikers

Although journalist participation had given the movement the impetus it needed to keep going until Gorbachev's visit, most of Beijing's citizens remained uninvolved. More important than the demonstrations of journalists and students, therefore, was the hunger strike begun on the Square on May 13 by about two thousand students. This brilliant tactical move finally released the spirit that had been bottled up for so long. A hunger strike is symbolically very powerful. A person who is willing to suffer death or, even worse, slow bodily decay because he or she refuses to eat the food produced by a society ruled by an unworthy government must be morally superior to ordinary humans, be they rulers or subjects. The immediate compassion felt for such a person, and the suspension of doubt about the validity of his or her cause, go together with the direct hatred felt for the government whose wickedness caused the hunger strike. Instead of being perceived as a calculated political act, the hunger strike is seen as the curse of the evil and powerful inflicted upon the just and powerless.

Within the political context of the People's Movement, the hunger strike was significant in that it provided the people with a depoliticized vehicle for political action. The hunger strike made it possible to demonstrate simply to support the hunger-striking students. It provided the spark, and the excuse, to express actively the long-felt sympathy for the students, born out of the dissatisfaction with the regime and its policies, through demonstrations that left this political message unstated. The message is quite simply that leaders who let hunger strikers die because of their refusal to talk with them are inhuman and unworthy to govern. On the one hand, this made it very difficult for the government to label the demonstrations counter-revolutionary and crack down on them. On the other hand, it made it possible for just about everybody, even party members in important party and government organizations, to demonstrate for the resignation of individual leaders, without raising doubts about their unflagging loyalty to the party and socialism.

The intellectuals were the first to realize the potential of the hunger strike. Some, such as Dai Qing, had been in regular contact with the students at least since early May and had played an important role in creating and maintaining a dialogue between them and party and state leaders. As a group, however, the intellectuals had shared most people's reservations about the student movement. Apart from their understandable fear of losing their jobs (intellectuals, too, have wives and children), the reforms had given them a place of some importance in the policy-making process. Many had the idea that their research and advice had been instrumental in deepening the reforms. They believed that the system could be changed from within, and that they had a role to play in that process. At the same time, however, they were extremely worried about the increased power of the conservatives among the party leadership, and their uncompromising attitude toward the students. They also realized that the student movement had deepened the rift within the top leadership between the conservatives and the pragmatic reformers. They knew that the next few days could decide the fate of the pragmatic reformers, and that the future of their own strategy of using the pragmatic reformers to press ahead with the reforms was at stake. The only hope for Zhao Ziyang and the other pragmatists was to use the movement as a political lever within the leadership. They needed to show that only a speedup of the reforms would satisfy the demonstrators.

When the hunger strike finally provided the opportunity to demonstrate, the intellectuals realized that it was up to them to set the example. The large demonstration of intellectuals on May 15 triggered off the massive demonstrations of May 17 and especially May 18 in which people from all walks of life participated. The intellectuals added a new, decisive element to the strategic and symbolic repertoire of the movement, which allowed it to grow into a genuine People's Movement. That the first demonstration of intellectuals happened on the day Gorbachev arrived in Beijing was of course no coincidence. It guaranteed maximum coverage by the domestic and foreign press, and severe loss of face for the Chinese government. The whole world was there to see that the Chinese authorities had lost control over their own capital. Not even a state visit of historical importance for China, and the supposed crowning of Deng Xiaoping as international statesman, could be carried out according to plan. Zhao himself was quick to rub this in when, on May 16, he told Gorbachev that it was still Deng Xiaoping who had the final say in all important policy matters.

The new, massive demonstrations followed the same pattern as the earlier demonstrations of students and journalists. The much larger numbers, however, meant that the problem of maintaining order became more acute. The students were forced into a new role, that of policeman. This also had an important symbolic value. First, it invalidated the government's rather transparent argument that the demonstrations had to be put to an end because they created chaos on and around the Square. Second, it showed that the city was no longer under the government's control, but that the students were the legitimate authority in Beijing. It was essential that demonstrators and bystanders behaved in an orderly fashion and complied voluntarily with the instructions of the student-policemen. In fact, as many people pointed out with a combination of glee and pride, under the students, Beijing was safe and orderly as never before.

As far as the demonstrations themselves were concerned, the most striking was the role of the work unit. As pointed out earlier, people demonstrated not as individuals, but as members of the delegation (literally "demonstration troops," *youxing duiwu*) of their work unit. These delegations in turn were often part of larger demonstrations of the "system" (*xitong*) or bureaucratic division to which the work unit belonged. System and work unit were almost always indicated by means of red banners with their names written in black or gold. Delegations were strictly segregated, and especially so from bystanders along the route. The first couple of weeks this was done by a ring of demonstrators walking hand in hand at the four sides of the demonstration (*shoulashou jiuchadui*). Later people started using colored strings held by the demonstrators at the edges of the delegation. Some of the better-organized delegations had two or more people walking ahead of the delegation ordering the bystanders to make way. The front section of the area sealed off by the ring of demonstrators was often left empty, with only one person wielding a banner or placard with demands or slogans, or a homemade satirical object (a marionette with Li Peng's face, a cartoon). Behind this person, two or three carried the identifying banner of the delegation, followed by a person (sometimes standing on the platform of a tricycle, and more often than not a young woman) rhythmically yelling the appropriate slogans of the day, which were repeated in chorus by the other members of the delegation.

The reasons for such a strict segregation of demonstrating delegations are complex. Most people said that it was needed to ensure order; otherwise, riotous elements could enter the demonstration and create trouble, providing the authorities with a perfect argument for forbidding the demonstrations. In my opinion, there was much more involved than that. A Chinese is first and foremost not an independent individual but a member of a family, a kin group, a village, and so forth. Within the group there is harmony, trust, and order. Outside the group, fear, cut-throat competition, and chaos reign supreme. Maintaining the boundary between the realms of harmony and chaos, between inside and outside, is an important preoccupation for almost every Chinese. Real or imagined, the demonstrators, too, saw the most immediate threat to their movement in the unpredictable mass of bystanders without identifiable social positions. Although the by-stander role was the most important political invention of the movement and its greatest source of strength, it was still treated with a distinctly Chinese fear of the unknown. Maintaining this strict separation between demonstrators and bystanders, however, even after the majority of the people of Beijing started demon-strating, proved to be an unexpected political resource, because it meant that one and the same individual could participate in the events in two different roles. After first having been "demon-strator" with other members of the work unit, one could return to the Square again, alone or with friends or family members, as bystander. The use and political force of this distinction only became clear to me after the proclamation of martial law on May 20 made demonstration impossible but could not curtail the con-tinuing support of the bystander.

The people of Beijing demonstrated in work-unit delegations for a number of complex reasons. I have already mentioned the dominant role of the work unit in all aspects of daily life in urban China. This is not only a consequence of the bureaucratic nature of China's social structure, but also because of the importance of the group in Chinese culture, which is reflected and strengthened by the modern work unit. The message the demonstrations were supposed to convey was that all of Chinese society had seen enough of the present leadership. To Chinese, society does not compromise all its citizens, but all groups and organizations that make it up. To be effective, the demonstrations had to be organ-ized by these groups and organizations, which in urban China meant the work units (and "systems").

The second reason for demonstrating in delegations was the fear of repercussions. By using the name of the unit, and partici-pating as a member of its delegation, one was no longer individu-ally responsible. Responsibility was shared with all other members and ultimately rested with the leader of the unit. Dem-onstrations in the unit's name needed either the permission or the passive consent of the unit's leader. If such consent was not given, enough pressure had to be exerted by the leader's superiors in the bureaucracy and/or by members of the unit themselves to neutralize the unit leader's opposition. The workers of the hotel where I was staying, for example, were forbidden by the unit's leader to demonstrate. They were told that the political risks for the unit (and presumably for the future career of the leader) would be too great. Instead, they had to be content with the role of bystander, which the leader did allow, and in any case could never have monitored effectively anyway. In this case, the workers were unable to overcome the opposition of their unit's leader. This probably had much to do with the fact that most employees were young girls working on contracts and thus had a very weak bargaining position vis-à-vis the leader. In many other cases, however, the balance of power was different, and leaders did allow demonstrations, or even organized some themselves. At the research institute that acted as my official host, most demonstrations were organized by self-appointed activists in the various research institutes of the same system. The leaders were content merely not to forbid their activities; something that also seems to have been the case with the journalists' demonstration of May 4. Two times (May 18 and May 24), however, the system and unit leaders officially sponsored the demonstrations, asking every unit to invite its members to participate. This is not to imply, however, that these demonstrations were identical to the pathetic attempts of the authorities during the last week of martial law to organize progovernment demonstrations. At my host unit, participation was always voluntary, and the demonstrations were organized by the leaders in order not to lose their credibility with members of the unit.

By stressing the crucial role of the unit and its leader in the development of the demonstrations, I do not mean to say that the demonstrations were orchestrated by members of the Zhao Ziyang faction in a last, desperate attempt to win what seemed to be a losing battle within the top leadership. To attribute all of the demonstrations to Zhao's influence does not fit well with the insistence of the student leaders and most Beijing citizens that they were spontaneous (*zifade*). Moreover, it greatly exaggerates the importance in Chinese society of the factional divisions among the top leadership. The people with whom I spoke almost never thought about ordinary individuals or units in terms of belonging to one faction or the other. Decisions by unit leaders to organize, allow, or oppose demonstrations are the result of weighing many factors against each other. The position of a unit leader is extraordinarily complicated and requires considerable political intelligence. On the one hand he or she is the leader of a unit, whose interests must be defended against other units and the higher levels of the bureaucracy. On the other hand, the leader is subordinate to these higher levels and has to appease their continuous pressure for compliance to their policies and targets. Added to this are the pressures applied through the informal network of personal connections the leader has built up to circumvent the inefficiencies of the rigid bureaucratic structure. A leader has to have the ability to balance all these interests and pressures without damaging his or her credibility with any of them. On top of that, he or she needs an almost intuitive sense of the political winds blowing through the bureaucracy and the top leadership in Beijing in order to be able to adjust policies in time to ensure that the unit and his or her own career survive the unceasing swings of the political pendulum. Personal loyalty to a higher-level leader, and through him or her perhaps a certain commitment to a particular faction at the top, may therefore be important but is by no means the only factor involved.

Zhao and his followers may have wanted to manipulate the movement for their own interests, but that alone can never explain the readiness of so many ordinary citizens to demonstrate. Within the units, tensions had been building up over the weeks, contained only by the political prudence the units' accumulated by unit members and leaders throughout a lifetime of political campaigns. The most probable reconstruction of what happened between May 15 and May 18 is that, when Zhao's supporters, through their personal connections, gave the green light to some selected units directly loyal to them (newspapers, research institutes, university staff, the Capital Iron and Steel Company), this unleashed a flood of other demonstrators. Because of the example set, these other unit leaders could no longer resist the pressure of ordinary members. At this juncture, many may even have judged it politically expedient to allow demonstrations; one does not want to seem too rash, but neither too conservative.

Zhao's influence over the movement was imperfect at best. This was also borne out by the fact that he was unable to stop the hunger strike and the demonstrations on May 17 and 18, when that would have given him a very powerful argument within the leadership. Once started, the demonstrations by the people gathered their own momentum and could not be stopped overnight. Another important factor was that the student movement had also experienced some important changes. Since the start of the hunger strike, students from outside Beijing had come into the capital. Many of the original Beijing student activists saw the dangers of continuing the hunger strike and staying on the Square: nourishing continued demonstrations would put the authorities increasingly on the defensive, perhaps sealing Zhao's fate, and leading to a violent confrontation instead of dialogue. These students were outweighed, however, by the newcomers who had not had their piece of the action. Moreover, within the student movement the hunger strikers had acquired great moral authority, which gave them absolute say over the whole movement. Cai Jinqing, at a conference at Brandeis University in September 1989, noted that students who did not participate in the hunger strike, who often were more moderate, found themselves completely dominated by those who did.

Paradoxically, only after Zhao had lost the power struggle at the top (effectively at a May 17 Politburo meeting at which he was the only one to oppose martial law) did his supporters get a firmer grip on the movement. His personal appearance at the Square on the morning of May 19, and especially the declaration of martial law that evening not by Zhao but by Li Peng, made it clear that Zhao had lost, and that the conservative victors were bent on cracking down hard on the movement. Only then did Zhao become the movement's hero and supposed savior of the nation. The progression of the demonstrators' slogans between May 15 and May 20 supports this reconstruction. The demonstrators' original demands were for the resignation (*cizhi*), dismissal (*xiatai*), or retirement (*lixiu*) primarily of Deng Xiaoping ("grandfather Deng is old, give him a plot of land in Sichuan [his home province] to retire to"), and secondarily of the group of leaders, including Zhao, who were responsible collectively for the government's refusal to talk to the students (collective resignation, *jiti cizhi*). After May 19, this was changed to the demand for the dismissal or downfall (*dadao*) of Li Peng, and then of Deng Xiaoping and Yang Shangkun. Another slogan called for the downfall of the "false government of Li Peng," implying that now a genuine government existed as well. Not only had the phrasing hardened, but individual leaders were singled out as well. The exception was Deng himself, who, as China's "little emperor," was thought to have a special personal responsibility from the beginning. The commitment of the movement to one of the factions within the leadership, a strategic pitfall the students had carefully avoided for so long, was a fact. This happened only after developments within the leadership itself left the movement with no other option. The strategy of forcing a dialogue with the leadership was bankrupt, and confrontation had become inevitable.

Phase Five: Martial Law and Suppression

After proclamation of martial law, it was impossible for most units to continue demonstrating. Demonstrating would now be illegal and would constitute an open challenge to the authorities. Only the groups that had been the first to demonstrate— journalists, students, and intellectuals—continued to do so. It was only after May 25 that the Center regained control over these units as well. Meetings of leaders within the units had to study the April 26 *People's Daily* editorial, which had condemned the student demonstrations as a "conspiracy." This prepared the way for a new anti–bourgeois liberalization campaign aimed at ferreting out the activists in each unit who had organized the demonstrations. The old system of political control had reasserted itself.

Meanwhile, very different things were happening on the streets, showing that the people had learned from their experiences. Although work-unit demonstrations were curtailed, the informal demonstrations of bystander support were beyond the reach of the work unit–centered control system. With the role of anonymous bystander, who had no identifiable place in the social and political structure, the term "the masses" gained real political content for the first time since the founding of the People's Republic. After martial law, the threat of an army invasion changed this passive, mandate-giving role into an active one: protector of the students at the Square.

The students themselves realized only too well that this was their last trump card. During the first two days after martial law was proclaimed, they devoted much of their energy to spreading propaganda among the people, asking them to leave their homes in the evening and assemble at street corners to block the army's path. An example is the following hand-copied message, one of the many the students distributed:

> SOS
> Dear Beijing, our beloved fatherland is in a most critical period now. It is possible that the field army sent by the government will already enter tonight. At this critical juncture, we urgently need the support and help of all citizens. We ask the citizens to go outside this evening. Save the students.
>
> —5/20

To bolster their appeal, the students spread the (probably incorrect) news that Deng Xiaoping and Li Peng had said that it would be permissible to kill twenty thousand people if this could insure twenty years of peace and order.

The people were forced to go to work, where they had to remain silent. But after work they cycled to the Square or simply stood guard at a street corner, waiting for the army to come. The following song was sung repeatedly by thousands who rode up and down Chang'an Avenue:

> Away with tiger Li;
> Day after day we will come;
> Those who rest at night will come by day;
> Those who rest by day will come at night.

Political control had rendered impossible the orderly and peaceful demonstrations to support the students and express dissatisfaction with the leadership. The students and the people had developed a way of making their voices heard without posing an immediate threat to the socialist system, but the leadership refused to understand this. Instead, they simply blocked this new communication channel. The frustrated citizens of Beijing had no other recourse but to assume the role of anonymous protector and confront the suppression head on. Until the last moment the citizens and students used nonviolent means to stop the army. They tried to convince "the soldiers, who are our sons and younger brothers," not to raise their weapons against their own people.

The leaders obviously did not have the intellectual and ideological flexibility to grasp correctly the significance of what was happening. They were prisoners of a world view that recognizes only three kinds of people—friends, enemies, and friends in need of correction—and elevates the leaders' own judgment to the level of absolute truth. Given their limitations they could probably react no other way. They only saw a lethal threat to their own power, and they defended that power in the same way they had gained it forty years earlier: by violence.

Conclusions

At the present time, it is impossible to know exactly what the significance of the movement will be for China's future. Some general remarks are possible, however.

First, the refusal of the leaders to talk to the students and the ensuing repression showed China's citizens that it is impossible to reform Chinese society under the continued leadership of the Communist Party. A confrontation with the party is inevitable if China is really to be remolded. The repression of the movement has sown the seeds of a future democratic system in China. Intellectuals, students, and workers now know why China needs democracy. Democracy, to the ordinary Chinese, is no longer an empty concept to be used as a rallying call for groups pressing for change, but a necessary condition to bring about real change in China.

Second, the key roles of students, intellectuals, and journalists in the development of the movement bridged the gap between scholars and the common people, which has been the traditional obstacle to so many past efforts to change China. The students and intellectuals who led the movement now have the mandate of the people and are the future leaders of the new China that they will create. Therefore, the political significance of the Democratic Front set up by refugees in Paris in September 1989 is not comparable to that of earlier refugee democratic organizations. Its leaders played crucial roles during the movement. The Chinese people will listen when they talk and act when they tell them to act. At present, China's political future is not made in China, but abroad.

Third, by combining the role of bystander with that of protector, the Chinese people have discovered a way to escape the unit-centered system of political control and the traditional particularism of Chinese culture. The role of the bystander is the germ of Chinese civil society, in which people will be able to act and organize as citizens, independent from the government bureaucratic structure.[4] Drawing on their experiences as bystander and protector, the people have become more than just occupants of a place in the bureaucratic structure or members of that gullible entity, "the masses." It was extremely significant that during the movement, and especially after martial law, people in the streets of Beijing had a strong sense of personal responsibility to maintain order. People were civil, considerate, and polite toward each other. The barrier separating the group from those outside it had come down, and new norms of public behavior had developed. No longer did I witness the usual fear of unknown outsiders, rudeness, and predation. Instead, a sense had developed that each individual citizen had his or her own dignity. Facing the common threat of the army, the people had discovered that they had something in common with all their fellow Chinese, and that they could relate to each other and cooperate as individuals, not only as members of different groups. It is unlikely that the people of Beijing will forget this profound experience. In the fight for, and construction of, a new democratic society, these newly discovered rights and duties as citizens, and the new norms of behavior that go with them, will prove to be the most important legacies of the Chinese People's Movement of 1989.

---

[4]Surprisingly enough, even leading individuals in the movement did not realize this aspect of the sympathy and protection offered by the bystanders, although they realized the crucial importance of building a new civil society. An example can be found in the June 2 "Declaration of Hunger Strike" by three intellectuals and one pop musician: "The student movement has won unprecedented sympathy, understanding, and support from every social group. The martial law has turned the democratic movement urged by the students into a movement urged by all the people. However, it is undeniable that many people support students out of their humanistic sympathy and discontent with the government. They lack civil consciousness with a sense of political responsibility. Therefore, we advocate that all the people have to give up the role of bystander and simply expressing sympathy, and should develop a sense of civic consciousness."

Five

PETITIONERS, POPPERIANS, AND HUNGER STRIKERS: THE UNCOORDINATED EFFORTS OF THE 1989 CHINESE DEMOCRATIC MOVEMENT

Woei Lien Chong

THE YEAR 1989 will be remembered in history as the blackest year in China since the reform program began in 1978. Nobody had foreseen that the peaceful actions started by the older generation of democrats and the students (each independent of the other) would lead to the horrible bloodshed witnessed in early June. With hindsight it can be concluded that the demonstrations fatally brought to a head three developments: the rift in the top leadership that had become apparent since autumn 1988, the discontent among the population about soaring inflation and bureaucratic corruption, and the disagreement at all levels of the party and government about how to solve China's political and economic crises.

The student demonstrations provided the citizens of Beijing with an opportunity to vent their grievances, and Premier Li Peng and his supporters apparently tried to convince Deng Xiaoping that party leader Zhao Ziyang was trying to harness the wave of popular unrest in order to seize power. By portraying Zhao as the mastermind behind the demonstrations, they used the student movement to tip the balance of power within the party in their own favor. As a warning to Zhao's supporters, the student demonstrations were denounced in the April 26 *People's Daily* editorial as "a counter-revolutionary plot." Zhao Ziyang refused to support this denunciation and opposed the subsequent plan to declare martial law announced on May 19.

After the massacre of early June, the hunt was on for leaders of the autonomous student and worker federations that had been established on Tiananmen Square, as well as for the intellectuals associated with Zhao and his reform policies, especially within the State Council's Research Institute for the Reform of the Economic Structure, the Chinese Academy of Social Sciences, and the Stone Corporation, a nonstate computer firm. Numerous people were arrested. In autumn 1989, the Rural Development Research Center also came under scrutiny. Zhao himself was relieved of all his posts, put under house arrest, and on July 5 accused of having conspired against Premier Li Peng. Rumors about an impending trial persisted until Zhao's house arrest was lifted in late October 1989. Apparently, it had been decided that he had been guilty of "errors," but not of criminal activities.

In late September 1989, a Front for a Democratic China (FDC) was established in France by exiled students and democratic leaders. This was a remarkable historical event, for three reasons: First, it clearly marked the end of the older intellectuals' previous hope that the Communist Party would be able to reform itself from within. Second, for the first time, the older intellectuals established their own political organization independent of the party, instead of working for reform from within party organs. Third, also for the first time, they cooperated with the students, whose actions, until then, had been separate from their own.

This chapter is an attempt to highlight, first, the difference between the student movement and the older intellectuals' petition movement, and second, the rift that arose between the dialogue-oriented student leaders, who were inspired by the philosopher Popper, and the radical hunger strikers, who were willing to become martyrs for the democratic cause.

The Call For Democracy

In January 1989, the well-known critical intellectual Fang Lizhi wrote an open letter to Deng Xiaoping, which started off a full-fledged petition movement. Many of the petitioners were inspired by the ideas and the example of Wei Jingsheng, the most prominent dissident of the Democracy Movement of 1978–79. In fact, Fang Lizhi had once declared himself a successor to Wei. Both the older democrats and the student leaders agreed with Wei that China's economic reforms could not succeed without a concomitant democratization of the political structure. This view was reinforced by the stagnation of the economic reforms in the 1980s. The democrats primarily ascribed this to widespread corruption and the unwillingness of the leadership to expand the private sector.

According to the democrats, the very same institutional and psychological conditions that led to the disastrous "Cultural Revolution" and previous mass campaigns are still present today: excessive concentration of power, lifelong tenure for politicians and officials, the absence of democratic and legal institutions to prevent and check abuses of power, the subservience of the media to politics, and the lack of a democratic tradition among the Chinese population. They feel that these same political factors also caused the present economic and political crises: the reforms have introduced economic decentralization in a political structure where popular and legal control on officials is virtually unknown. The combination of increased economic liberty with continued political repression, it is said, has led to the widespread corruption and graft among party and government officials that is one of the main sources of popular anger.

To protect the position of the party, Deng Xiaoping has refused to liberalize the political system. Apart from the fact that Deng, as a firm Leninist, is convinced of the necessity to maintain the Communist Party's leadership, he has had to safeguard his delicate alliance with the veteran leaders who supported his comeback and his ousting of the "Gang of Four." These veteran leaders were willing to support Deng's economic reforms to a certain extent, but they resolutely opposed any measures that would undermine the party's monopoly of power. Deng only tolerated the Democracy Movement of 1978–79 as long as he could use it as an instrument in the power struggle against his opponents within the party. Once firmly on top, he lost no time in formulating the limits of his political tolerance. Criticism was not to pass beyond the threshold of the so-called Four Principles: adherence to socialism, the leadership of the party, the democratic dictatorship of the proletariat, and Marxism-Leninism and Mao Zedong Thought.

In the economic field, experimentation with market mechanisms was only allowed within the limits of the planned economy and the existing political system. Independent of the Soviet model and the Maoist past, China would create its own "socialism with Chinese characteristics." Thus, Deng consolidated his alliance with the ideologically conservative veterans. As a result of this political compromise, the position of artists and intellectuals did not structurally improve. Periods of cultural thaw alternated with periods of repression, in which campaigns were launched to purify the cultural ranks from the contamination of "pernicious Western ideas," such as the anti–spiritual pollution campaign in 1983–84.

This campaign was cut short by Hu Yaobang, then party general secretary, and himself an advocate of cultural and intellectual liberalization. It was clear that the continued practice of political mass campaigns did not contribute to the creation of the stable political atmosphere needed for economic reforms, and it was feared that agricultural production would be endangered if the peasants became involved in the campaign. Beating a temporary retreat, the conservatives decided to take revenge on Hu as soon as they found an opportunity. The occasion came with the student demonstrations of late 1986. Hu was accused of having been too lenient in ideological and other political matters and was dismissed as party leader, although he retained his seat in the Politburo. Another ideological campaign was launched, against so-called bourgeois liberalization. Academics, artists, and intellectuals once again were faced with censorship and intimidation.

1989: Climax of Events

In his open letter to Deng Xiaoping of January 6, Fang Lizhi requested the release of all Chinese political prisoners, especially Wei Jingsheng. He said that 1989 was a suitable year to declare an amnesty, since it was an important anniversary year for the founding of the People's Republic of China (1949), the May Fourth Movement (1919), the French Revolution (1789), and the imprisonment of dissident Wei Jingsheng (1979). Following his example, many older intellectuals signed petitions aimed at exerting pressure on the National People's Congress (NPC), which convened in March–April. It was hoped that the delegates would prepare an amnesty and make proposals for democratization. The older democrats complained about corruption, inflation, the lack of press freedom, and political interference in education, science, literature, and the arts. Moreover, requests were made to increase investment in education and research, and to improve the appalling housing and financial conditions of intellectuals.

Much to the annoyance of the leadership, the NPC accepted a petition presented by a Hong Kong delegation, which had arrived at Tianjin airport on March 28, signed by twenty-four thousand people all over the world in support of the Chinese petition movement. The petition's acceptance, in defiance of the government's refusal to allow the delegation to leave the airport, was a clear indication that the petition movement had found support among some of the NPC delegates.

The campus of Beijing University also stirred with political activities. On April 3, a big character poster was put up by fifty-six students, echoing Fang Lizhi's call to make the university into a special zone for promoting democratic politics. On April 5, the official anniversary of the end of the "Cultural Revolution," hundreds of students ignored a prohibition on assembly and held a meeting at which Li Shuxian delivered a speech calling on the students to support democracy, which, she said, was a fundamental human right. The meeting was followed by a march to Tiananmen Square, but the students found that it had been closed off by a large police presence.

Thus, weeks before Hu Yaobang's death, the authorities were faced with student activism in addition to the wave of petitions initiated by the older intellectuals, and they took strong measures to check both movements. On the same day that the army closed off Tiananmen Square to the marching students, the authorities had, in Shanghai, detained activist Chen Jun. Chen was one of the leaders of the petition movement and founder of "Amnesty '89," an "independent organization for investigating the situation of political prisoners," established in February 1989 during the petition movement. Chen Jun has ties with the China Alliance for Democracy (CAD) in New York, which publishes the "subversive" magazine *China Spring*. On April 8, Chen arrived in San Francisco, saying that the Chinese authorities had thrown him out of the country.

The situation was further complicated when the leader of a CAD offshoot, Wang Bingzhang, arrived in Tokyo from the United States, reportedly with the intention of joining the student demonstrations that had started after Hu Yaobang's death on April 15. The heightened activity of prominent anti-CCP dissident leaders from the ranks of CAD aroused the suspicion of the authorities, although neither the petitioners nor the students raised antiparty slogans.

The students had not participated in the petition movement, but following the death of Hu Yaobang they organized spontaneous demonstrations, partly out of grief for the deceased former party leader, partly out of disappointment about the outcome of the NPC, which had taken no steps to further democratization. Hu had died of a heart attack less than two-and-a-half years after his conservative opponents had forced him to resign as party leader in January 1987. Because he had been accused of being responsible for the student demonstrations of late 1986, his death made him a martyr for the democratic cause. The students demanded his rehabilitation, an investigation into corruption and inflation, and educational reforms. The government realized that the protests by intellectuals and students found approval among large sections of the population, whose standard of living had been deteriorating as a result of high inflation, low productivity, and the rampant corruption of party and government officials. Bureaucrats fueled inflation by buying large quantities of goods at low, state-fixed prices and selling them again at much higher market prices, pocketing huge profits. Moreover, it was these same bureaucrats on whom common workers and citizens depended for the distribution of jobs and housing, permits to marry and give birth to a child, and so forth—"favors" that are seldom granted for nothing. While many people in recent years faced decreasing incomes or even unemployment, bureaucrats drove around in luxurious imported cars and built themselves multi-storied villas. No wonder that the student call "Down with corruption!" was wholeheartedly supported by the population of Beijing, and by a considerable number of people within the party and state organizations themselves. Thus, the conservative leaders were not predominantly worried about the actual events in the Square, but about the unity of the party and their own power position within it. They apparently decided to make it unambiguously clear to Zhao's supporters that he was on the losing side, and that political reform was out of the question; thus, the hard-line editorial of April 26.

The older democrats immediately came out to support the students, marching on May 15 and 18 in protest against the government's denunciation of the student movement and in support of the hunger strike, which had started on May 13. A written testimony of support was delivered in the "May 17 Manifesto," signed by, among others, Yan Jiaqi, Bao Zunxin, and Li Nanyou.

The manifesto demanded the abolition of the dictatorship and the gerontocracy, denying that the student movement was a "rebellion," and calling it instead "a great patriotic and democratic movement for the ultimate burial of dictatorship and feudalism in China."

The difference between the petition movement and the student movement was obscured by the fact that they followed closely upon each other chronologically, and that many older intellectuals rallied to the support of the students in May. Nevertheless, the movements had separate backgrounds and objectives and were organized independently from one another.

Separate Backgrounds

Beside age, the differences separating the students from the older democrats were manifold. First and foremost, there was the difference in social position. Most older intellectuals had been rehabilitated under Deng Xiaoping, after their persecution by Mao Zedong during the antirightist campaign of 1957 for their criticism of the Chairman's policies. They tried to work for reform from within the institutions in which they had found new positions, while the students still stood outside the established social structures in terms of power and influence.

Moreover, the older intellectuals entertained a long-term, institutional view of democratization. They hoped that the party's power monopoly would be gradually undermined by developments in the economic and educational fields. The economic reforms would, in spite of the leadership's aversion to such a phenomenon, lead to the rise of an indigenous middle class, who would eventually demand the political power to match their economic position. Fang Lizhi expected all this to happen within twenty or thirty years. Meanwhile, many intellectuals felt they had a responsibility to change the submissive attitude of the Chinese population toward power and authority, by pointing out fundamental social and economic problems and articulating demands for democratization and human rights within the limits of the Chinese Constitution, through speeches, open letters, and petitions.

Third, the older intellectuals realized that the reform process in China had been initiated, not by a popular movement, but by the top leadership under Deng Xiaoping. As a top-down managed process, it would remain strongly dependent upon individual reformist leaders for a long time to come. The older democrats wanted to support the reformist leaders without endangering the stability of the entire party and governmental apparatus. The petition movement of January–March 1989 was intended as a sign of support for the proreform leaders, while avoiding undermining the party's legitimacy or competing with it in organizing the population. The petition movement was not aimed at establishing independent organizations of pressure groups. It was only on May 23, in the wake of the student movement, that a number of older intellectuals, led by Yan Jiaqi, established the "Beijing Intellectuals' Autonomous Association."

The students, on the other hand, had informally founded the "Beijing Students' Autonomous Federation" on April 21, shortly after Hu Yaobang's death. Moreover, they raised different demands: they did not focus on the release of political prisoners, the central theme of the petition movement. They demanded official recognition for their own independent student organizations; although they avoided attacking the system in so many words, their initiatives in self-organization were a threat to the system. Originally, it seemed as if the three main student leaders—Wu'er Kaixi, Wang Dan, and Shen Tong—were well in control of the movement. But after the hunger strike began on May 13, the atmosphere in the Square quickly became radicalized, and the three leaders were fatally estranged from the hunger strikers.

The Cleavage within the Student Movement

On May 13, the student leaders began a hunger strike in the Square to increase the pressure on the government, but they knew full well that the Square would have to be cleared before Soviet leader Mikhail Gorbachev would make his appearance there on May 15. The student movement became divided over the issue of whether to withdraw before May 15 or not. The three main student leaders realized that staying beyond that date would mean a scandalous loss of face for the government and inevitable repression of their movement. The radical students, eventually to be led by Chai Ling, wanted to continue the hunger strike to the bitter end. While the former had a well-defined plan of action and concrete objectives, the latter did not.

Wu'er Kaixi, Wang Dan, and Shen Tong wanted to change Chinese political procedures by establishing a constructive dialogue with the government about China's social and political future. To achieve this purpose, they cooperated with reformist older intellectuals and were willing to support Zhao Ziyang's position in the leadership, after he had shown his support to the students by opposing Li Peng's denunciation of their movement. In contrast, the hunger strikers were not interested in supporting any one leader in a power struggle against the others, and it appears that they had no concrete political alternative. They would probably have accepted Li Peng's leadership and the power monopoly of the party, if only their demands had been met. They refused to listen to the urgent pleas of the three main leaders and older intellectuals to leave the Square before May 15, and they decided to stay even after the announcement of martial law on May 19. They said that leaving the Square would be a loss of face for the students. They were firmly resolved to continue their peaceful demonstration and, if need be, sacrifice their lives for the cause of democracy. By this historical deed, they said that they wanted to arouse the Chinese population from its political slumber. Their heroic intransigence caused the government to lose face in front of the assembled international press, and this was one of the reasons why the three student leaders' attempt to establish a structural dialogue came to nothing. On June 3 and 4, tanks and armed soldiers washed away the leaders' shame with the blood of unarmed students and civilians.

The Popperians' Original Action Program

For a number of years, the three main student leaders had been contemplating the problems of Chinese society within the independent study groups they had set up. Wu'er Kaixi's "Confucius Study Society" at Beijing Normal University was concerned with educational problems, and Wang Dan had established a "democratic salon" that convened every Wednesday afternoon on the campus of Beijing University to debate political affairs. Every Wednesday evening on the same campus, Shen Tong's "Olympic Science Academy" discussed problems in the philosophy of science, after Shen had opened the session by reading a piece by Karl Popper. The writings of the vehemently antitotalitarian philosopher convinced Shen and his colleagues that open, rational dialogue was the key to both the growth of knowledge and democratic politics.

Popper's popularity in China was due to his attack on Marxism as a "pseudo-science," on the basis of methodological and logical arguments. In China, Marxism has not only long been regarded as unassailable scientific truth (a contradiction in terms, Popper would say), but even has been elevated to the status of a super-science, serving as the touchstone for all scientific theories. Popper forcefully pointed out that the reinforcing of dogma has nothing to do with science, since it does not provide new knowledge but only reaffirms what is already claimed to be known. The true scientist does not seek evidence to prove that he or she is right, since positive evidence can be found for all kinds of contradictory theories—which means that even an increasing amount of positive evidence does not guarantee that a theory is true. Instead, the only genuinely scientific method is to do one's utmost to prove that one is *wrong*. New knowledge is only achieved by formulating daring hypotheses and the sustained attempt to test them, in an effort to prove them false. It is logically impossible, says Popper, to demonstrate that an empirical hypothesis is true, but if it is false, then this can be conclusively shown.[1] Popper used the falsifiability of hypotheses as a criterion to demarcate scientific hypotheses from nonscientific ones: only hypotheses that are formulated in such a way that they can be refuted are scientific. Hypotheses that are unrefutable (and thus, in Popper's definition, untestable) are not scientific. The total body of knowledge grows by the discarding of the "falsified" hypotheses, not by the reinforcing of established dogma.[2]

In other words, Popper stood on their head dominant traditional notions about science, providing the Chinese students with a powerful intellectual weapon to dismiss the party's claim that Marxism-Leninism is the one and only true science—indeed, Popper's initial position was that it is not a science at all.[3] This meant that, among Chinese students in the 1980s, Popper had succeeded in his intention of undermining the epistemological prop legitimating the power of the Communist Party.[4]

Moreover, Popper provided the students not only with an alternative methodology, but also with an alternative political theory. The growth of knowledge, according to Popper, presupposes a free social and political atmosphere in which daring hypotheses can be formulated without fear, tested without prejudice, and, if proven false, discarded without qualms. It presupposes the possi-

---

[1]In reaction to critics, Popper later modified his view on the "fail-safe" character of the refutation method. Still, he maintained the principle of refutability ("the falsifiability principle") both as the cornerstone of his methodology and as the demarcation principle between "science" and "pseudo-science."

[2]Karl Popper, *The Logic of Scientific Discovery* (New York: Harper and Row, 1968). Chinese academic methodologists are well aware of the debate between Popper and Thomas Kuhn on the structure of scientific activity. For Kuhn's view, see his *Structure of Scientific Revolutions* (Chicago: University of Chicago Press, 1962).

[3]Later, he changed his mind and held that Marxism *was* a scientific theory, but one offering hypotheses that had already been refuted by the facts.

[4]Karl Popper, *The Open Society and Its Enemies* (parts 1 and 2), 5th rev. ed. (London: Routledge and Kegan Paul, 1980). Even Chinese writers on Popper who do not refer to this work clearly know its main thesis.

bility of open, free, and rational discussion, which only exists, he said, in a political structure where the population is in possession of orderly procedures to remove the government: a "democracy," in Popper's definition. In contrast, the growth of knowledge cannot proceed under "tyranny," which Popper defines as a political system in which the population cannot remove the government through orderly means and is therefore unfree. Popper's concept of rational dialogue inspired the action program of the 1989 student movement, as formulated by Shen Tong, Wang Dan, and Wu'er Kaixi.

The three young men, for the same reasons as those presented by the leaders of the petition movement, agreed that 1989 was a suitable year to organize joint actions. They had not yet decided on what actions to take when Hu Yaobang unexpectedly died on April 15 and a great number of students took to the streets. The three campus celebrities immediately realized that this was the ideal opportunity to start a full-fledged movement, and they soon succeeded in being elected as its leaders. Initially, however, the students objected to Wang Dan assuming a leading role, since his name was associated with that of Fang Lizhi and Li Shuxian and they did not want to give the impression that the students were under Fang's command.

The three student leaders had a clear strategy with precisely formulated objectives. First, they wanted gradually to increase the pressure on the government, with demonstrations followed by strikes and then by a hunger strike, in order to establish a dialogue with the leadership. Second, once this aim had been reached, the students would return to the campuses and transform them into democratic strongholds, continuing their radio stations and newspapers, and further developing their students' federation. Every Chinese university was to establish its own independent and autonomous movement "to create the largest possible scope for freedom." Finally, the moment would arrive at which all students from all over China would come out in a nationally coordinated action, "to push the conservative wing aside."

The May 14 Meeting

Things did not go as planned, however. The government's April 26 editorial left no doubt about the leadership's refusal to enter into dialogue with an organization it deemed illegal. On May 4, however, after party leader Zhao Ziyang returned from his trip to North Korea, he called for a general dialogue. The leadership committee (presided over by Li Peng) that had previously dealt with the students was dissolved, and a preparatory meeting was held on May 8 between the students' "Dialogue Delegation," established by Shen Tong on May 3, and the head of the State Education Commission, Li Tieying.

Wu'er Kaixi established a committee to prepare the actual dialogue, consisting of himself and thirty of the most prominent academics and intellectuals, including specialists in constitutional law. The committee worked for a fortnight to design a plan for China's future society, with each member calling on the staff of his university to provide the necessary documents and statistics. Meanwhile, the reformists appointed Wan Runnan, president of China's biggest nonstate computer firm, the Stone Corporation, as an intermediary between Zhao's reformers and the students. During a meeting on May 13 with Yan Mingfu, head of the United Front Work Department, it was agreed that the students would evacuate the Square on two conditions: (1) an official retraction of the April 26 editorial was to be issued, and (2) the discussion would be broadcast live on television.

On May 14, the long-awaited dialogue was held, chaired by Li Tieying. Li was seconded by a minister and ten vice-ministers. Wu'er Kaixi had brought, apart from Shen Tong, Wang Dan, and Chai Ling, a delegation of twelve intellectuals from his preparatory committee. Wu'er Kaixi's delegation wanted to discuss three main themes, divided over twenty-nine chapters: legalization and general recognition of the Students' Autonomous Federation, the reforms, and paragraph thirty-five of the Chinese Constitution, concerning civil rights. When an official announced that the meeting could not be broadcast directly, "for technical reasons," it was agreed that every half hour, a tape would be taken to the television station to be broadcast.

Break Down the Doors!

The discussion started and continued until a crowd of two thousand hunger strikers arrived at the premises and tried to break down the doors. They were alarmed because nothing had appeared on television, and it was rumored that their leaders were talking with the government behind their backs. Wu'er Kaixi went downstairs and tried to talk to the angry crowd, to persuade them to let the meeting continue undisturbed, but he spoke in vain. People moved past him, kicked down the doors, ran up the stairs, and broke into the meeting, demanding that the dialogue be broadcast. At that moment, the student leaders realized that both they and the ministers had been framed. Zhao's opponents had never intended to broadcast the meeting—they had wanted the dialogue to fail, so that the Square would not be evacuated before Gorbachev's arrival, and Zhao's political fate would be sealed. Shen Tong slammed the table with his fist and burst into tears: he and the entire movement had failed utterly and completely. This fiasco was a harbinger of the repression that he knew would inevitably come. Devastated, the three student leaders left the building at midnight.

Gorbachev was due to arrive in the Square within a few hours. The three decided that the Square had to be cleared as quickly as possible. They explained the situation to the students there, emotionally apologizing for their failure, but the students refused to budge. Wu'er Kaixi then said that they could try to move everyone to the eastern side of the Square so that they would be out of sight of the cameras when Gorbachev entered the Square from the western side. Throughout the night, the three talked to all the university leaders in the tents, and to the hunger strikers. Finally, at dawn, everyone started to pack and prepared to leave. The three thought that they had succeeded in averting disaster, but they looked about and suddenly saw an immense crowd of hundreds of thousands of students, workers, and citizens of Beijing flooding the Square in support of the movement. Horrified, Shen Tong realized that rational control over the movement had become impossible, and that it had developed its own uncontrollable momentum. The worst was yet to come. His carefully planned strategy lay in ruins. He cried like a child. It was all over.

The Meeting with Li Peng

But Wu'er Kaixi still had hope. On May 18, he escaped from the hospital where he had been taken after collapsing with fatigue. Still dressed in his pajamas, he went to the meeting with Li Peng, who had finally agreed to a discussion. When Li Peng started a rambling monologue, Wu'er Kaixi unabashedly interrupted, repeating that the students would only leave the Square if the April 26 editorial was retracted and a genuine dialogue established on equal terms. Li Peng, insulted and intransigent, demanded that the Square be evacuated and refused to discuss Wu'er Kaixi's terms. As the students angrily reproached the Premier, Wu'er Kaixi suddenly fell to the floor, gasping for breath. Li Peng left. Wu'er Kaixi, suffering from an apparent heart attack, was taken to the hospital, and the meeting ended inconclusively.

While Wu'er Kaixi was out of action, the movement in the Square came under Chai Ling's leadership. Her colleagues compiled a new list of demands and announced that the movement had now embarked on a more radical course. In the night of May 19–20, Li Peng declared martial law. Hearing this, Wu'er Kaixi again escaped from the hospital and went to the Square. He sought out four other student leaders to support his plan to order an evacuation—one too few to make the decision binding for the whole movement. Breaking the rules, he spoke over the microphone and ordered an evacuation. As a result, he was subsequently dismissed as chair of the students' federation. Now, the students were in the hands of fate.

At 11:00 P.M. on June 3, Wu'er Kaixi was heading the students' disciplinary marshals, trying to find out what was happening in the city with the arrival of the army, when his heart again failed him. He was taken to the hospital by the last ambulance at 2:00 A.M. He was later smuggled out of Beijing and appeared in Paris on July 4. Shen Tong, rescued by Beijing citizens from the massacre raging in the Xidan District in the night of June 3, arrived in the United States. Wang Dan was arrested in Beijing in mid-June, and there was no trace of Chai Ling until she appeared in Paris in May 1990.

Problems in Exile: Differences within the FDC

The early June massacre has convinced even cautious intellectuals like Liu Binyan, Su Shaozhi, and Yan Jiaqi that reform of China's political system from within is impossible. Fang Lizhi, Yan said, had been quicker than they to realize this. Together with Wu'er Kaixi and Stone's former president Wan Runnan, they established the FDC to prepare for the creation of a multiparty system within China after the fall of Li Peng. It is emphasized, however, that the FDC is not itself a political party, let alone an opposition party. The FDC has vowed never to use violent means to achieve its aims, and it hopes that it can enter into dialogue with the Communist Party in an attempt to make it share power with other parties.

Members of the FDC hope that continued developments in the economic and educational spheres will lead to the rise of a middle class who will eventually demand the political power to match their economic position. This, in combination with international sanctions against the Li Peng government and the gradual spreading in China of the true story of the 1989 events, will make a violent overthrow of the party unnecessary. "The force of economics and information," says Wan Runnan, "is stronger than that of guns." The older intellectuals remain committed to a policy of nonviolence and a belief in the necessity of rational dialogue.

In this context, the events in 1989 have raised one crucial question: Is an open dialogue on equal terms feasible in a totalitarian political culture in which the "face" of all-powerful individual leaders is crucial? Since the student leaders had been inspired by Popper, it must be noted that the spirited philosopher has never addressed this question directly.

As mentioned above, Karl Popper defended "democracy" against "tyranny" from the point of view of scientific progress. A "democracy," Popper said, is more conducive to the growth of knowledge than is "tyranny," because the latter cannot guarantee the free, rational discussion necessary for the quest for scientific truth, while a "democracy" can. This is not the same, however, as saying that a tyranny can be transformed by rational discussion, which was the way the Chinese student leaders interpreted his work. Popper regarded himself as a philosopher of science, not a political philosopher. He only stated what he found was the most suitable political structure for the growth of knowledge; he did not specifically address practical problems of reform in totalitarian systems.

In the well-known debate with the philosopher Herbert Marcuse, Popper defended the thesis that capitalist society can be reformed by nonviolent, piecemeal measures, making use of pre-existing democratic political institutions. Marcuse doubted the efficacy of politics, in view of what he called the "totalitarian" nature of consumerist capitalist society, and advocated a social revolution. In this debate, Popper came forward in defense of "reform within the system," but it should be noted that the debate was about Western capitalist society, not the Marxist-Leninist party-state.

Among the members of FDC, different viewpoints have arisen concerning the issues of violence versus nonviolence, social evolution versus revolution, and dialogue with the CCP versus opposition to the CCP. This internal disagreement reflects the contrast between the moderate stance of the FDC leaders toward the CCP and the radical, antisystem attitude of leading figures in the New York-based CAD.

The FDC and CAD are reported to be divided over tactics. The various groups within CAD are in favor of "reform outside the system"; they oppose the power monopoly of the party and even intend to wrest power from it. In contrast, it is said, the FDC aims at "reform within the system," expecting that a moderate faction will ascend to power in Beijing and rehabilitate the democratic movement, and even eventually establish political plurality. It should be noted that the continued use of the term "reform within the system" is misleading, for it has taken on a new meaning since June 1989. Previously, it denoted the older intellectuals' preference to work for reform from within established institutions, without overtly attacking the CCP's power monopoly. Now, since the FDC does openly attack the monolithic party-state, the term is used to describe the moderates' policy of aiming at a dialogue with the CCP, to persuade it to accept a multiparty system and a market economy. Before, older intellectuals did not advocate the establishment of an opposition party. Now they do, but the moderates want to postpone the actual establishment until some convenient time in the future, to diminish the direct threat posed to the CCP. The FDC, while attacking the Li Peng government, refrains from antagonizing the CCP as such, keeping open the roads to dialogue and compromise. It has declared that it wants to terminate the one-party dictatorship, not by overthrowing the ruling CCP, but by preparing the way to a multiparty system by peaceful means.

Other exiled activists have different views, both on the issue of an opposition party and on the use of violence. Former CAD leader Wang Bingzhang is convinced that the time is ripe for establishment of an opposition party and he has already taken the initiative. He emphasized that he is not out to destroy the CCP and "will always provide it with the opportunity to function as one party among a variety of parties." Both he and trade union leader Qiu Wu take into account that the use of violence might eventually prove unavoidable, in view of the violent and totalitarian nature of the present regime. In the words of Qiu Wu, "a peaceful reform of this system is an intellectuals' illusion." He is thinking in terms of an organized armed uprising of short duration to overthrow the CCP.

These debates demonstrate that Chinese democrats are still divided about the question of whether or not the totalitarian Chinese party-state can be transformed by a nonviolent, evolutionary process, and on the basis of rational dialogue. There are signs that both moderates and radicals, over the short term, believe in the likelihood of a national economic collapse, large-scale popular unrest, political paralysis of the center, regional and provincial opposition against Beijing, and perhaps even a power struggle after the death of Deng Xiaoping. Speculatively speaking, at bottom the differences between moderates and radicals revolve around the question of whether the CCP, faced with social and economic catastrophe, will show itself willing to make concessions, notably the establishment of a multiparty system and a market economy, in return for outside help in restabilizing the political situation in China. On this question, the moderates are more optimistic than the radicals.

Six

THE EMERGENCE OF CIVIL SOCIETY IN CHINA, SPRING 1989

Lawrence R. Sullivan

No Man is under an obligation to obey any but the legitimate powers of the state.

—Jean Jacques Rousseau

THE PRODEMOCRACY demonstrations in Beijing and other cities from April to June 1989 were more than just an episodic expression of popular discontent with the Chinese government. Perhaps more than any previous movement in modern Chinese history, the mass participation of Chinese people from a variety of occupations and the genuine good feeling that animated most of the participants before the crackdown of June 3 and 4 indicated that a fundamental transformation of popular consciousness took place among the urban population. Of prime importance was the non-violent nature of the protests. The extraordinary self-discipline of the one-million-strong demonstrations was a testimony to the population's collective awareness that violence would only destroy the movement's moral force.

During the Cultural Revolution China's leaders, especially Mao Zedong, fostered profound distrust and mutual suspicion among the population by cynically manipulating popular discontent and encouraging internecine strife for their narrow ideological goals. In contrast, 1989 witnessed the formation of a genuine civil society in urban China as mutual bonds and a collective popular consciousness were created among disparate groups and individuals.[1] Whereas previous demonstrations and calls for democracy, such as in late 1986, engendered little popular reaction, the massive support for the student movement in 1989 indicated a profound rupture between state and society and a major breakdown in longstanding divisions between intellectuals and the "people." As this essay demonstrates, the distrust and animosity that have divided intellectuals and students from workers and "city residents" (shi min) disintegrated in reaction to government intransigence and the top leadership's self-imposed isolation. Popular fears of social "chaos" (luan) and mutual class antagonism—often cultivated by the Communist leadership to maintain supreme authority—rapidly eroded as the populace declared independence from the omnipresent state and embraced the students, especially the hunger strikers, as the embodiment of the popular will. In one fell swoop, Chinese urban society, particularly in Beijing, was transformed from a "sheet of loose sand" (yipan sansha) into a cohesive civil society capable of maintaining social order and even assuming the everyday functions of government without "central" control. Although the popular movement was ultimately crushed by the military crackdown, the galvanizing of an embryonic general will and popular sovereignty is a legacy of the spring demonstrations that probably cannot be easily erased even by coercion and government propaganda.

Rousseau and Civil Society

For Jean Jacques Rousseau, the creation of civil society (or, "civil state") was the fundamental prerequisite for democratic government. As a mere "agglomeration," men were susceptible to the rule of tyrants, but once constituted as an "association,"

---

[1] Although peasant participation in the demonstrations did occur in Beijing and other cities, rural reaction to the spring upheaval was limited. Demonstrations in Nanjing and relatively small cities, such as occurred in Anhui Province, however, involved some peasant participation.

the people were transformed into a "moral and collective body" separate from the absolutist state. Whereas under absolutism the individual was obsessed with maximizing his or her self-interest and was oblivious to the common good, now he or she would "realize that he is under compulsion to obey quite different principles, and that he must . . . consult his reason and not merely respond to the promptings of desire." "Justice and utility" were no longer separated, for in the "civil state" individuals were intimately aware of the consequence of their actions for the entire body politic. Under absolutism, every person was a "slave" attached to a particular "master" in what, above all, was a highly personalistic authority structure that made the formation of civil society a virtual impossibility. Personalism and absolutism were, for Rousseau (and also Montesquieu), mutually reinforcing attributes of a society in which powerful despots ruled over self-serving, egotistical men who were incapable of collective action. But in civil society, "each person gives himself to all and not to any one individual," thereby creating a universal sense of obligation and belief that one "owes a duty to each of his neighbors." The interminable struggle for survival and personal gain characteristic of a mere "agglomeration" is replaced by a common awareness of mutual interest and capacity for unified action against the absolutist state. Indeed, Rousseau believed civil society was characterized by an organic unity so that "any attack upon one of its members is [considered] an attack upon itself." Man in civil society is both rational and civilized: "For to be subject to appetite is to be a slave, while to obey laws laid down by society is to be free."[2]

Unlike Karl Marx, Rousseau did not believe that the formation of civil society was a culmination of a long process of historical or material development. Writing in the mid-eighteenth century

---

[2] See Jean Jacques Rousseau, *Social Contract*, excerpted in Hanna Fenichel Pitkin, *Representation* (New York: Atherton Press, 1969), pp. 54–55 and 58; and *The Social Contract, or the Principles of Political Right* (New York: Hafner Publishing Co., 1947).

(and still reflecting lingering influences of the French Enlightenment), Rousseau saw few prerequisites to the emergence of a cohesive popular consciousness, certainly nothing so substantial as Marx's requirements of a comprehensive change in economic production and property systems. For Rousseau, the "common interest," which makes the establishment of civil society possible, merely necessitated a relatively equal property ownership and a general consensus that collective action was vital for individual "preservation." The act by which a people constitute themselves as such was a spontaneous expression of will, driven by a widespread desire of people to assert their "quality" as civilized human beings against the drudgery and degradation of slavery under absolutism. Compared to the rather conservative thrust of Marx's historical materialism ("conservative" in the sense that an orthodox reading of Marx would argue against rapid changes in popular consciousness), Rousseau's vision was a fundamentally radical one. Civil society and the resultant capacity to express the general will as sovereign authority could literally come on a moment's notice, just as it did in China in spring 1989.[3]

Civil Society and the Chinese Popular Movement

> Mao Zedong treated the Chinese people like children.
> —Chinese intellectual, summer 1988

The emergence of civil society as defined by Rousseau was readily apparent in China during spring 1989, especially after the inauguration of the student hunger strike in mid-May. Although the massive show of collective will on Beijing's streets was undoubtedly influenced by the economic reforms begun in

---

[3] The failure of Western China specialists, and even the Chinese student organizers, to predict a popular outpouring of support demonstrated this fact. Fang Lizhi was the only person to foresee the upcoming political earthquake in January 1989. See Fang Lizhi, "China Needs Democracy," *Liberation*, January 17, 1989, in *FBIS-China*, January 27, 1989.

the late 1970s, Chinese society's sudden separation from the state's embrace was an unprecedented development in the history of the PRC. Social unity now replaced class divisions and mutual suspicions as the major theme in student, worker, and citizen pronouncements. The "dog-eat-dog" character of life in Beijing rapidly gave way to a social graciousness and common concern for individual welfare that surprised Chinese and foreign observers alike. That the population asserted its political "sovereignty" was also evident in the rapid assumption of mundane state functions such as traffic and crime control. When local pickpockets openly announced a halt to their nefarious activities, it was just another demonstration that the people could achieve the common good *better* than the vast state and police apparati. Although the prospects for long-term self-management were undoubtedly limited, the few days in which the citizenry assumed responsibility for maintaining social order sent a message to political authorities that the population was not the helpless and "childlike" mass that the leadership assumes in justifying its dictatorship. Beijing and other cities became a giant political stage in which the people proved to their absolutist and patriarchal leaders that self-government in China was not just a demand, but already a reality.

This assertion of self-rule reflected an unprecedented expression of Chinese society's separation from the omnipresent state. In public pronouncements and incipient organizations, China's students, workers, businessmen, and even some peasants declared their independence from the vast bureaucratic apparatus. This was not only apparent in the widespread use of the term "autonomous" (*zizhi*) by student groups, unions, and various "citizen groups," but also in statements that clearly distinguished between "those who rule and those who are ruled."[4] Whereas in previous demonstrations, such as the 1976 April

---

[4] Beijing Workers' Autonomous Federation (BWAF), "Letter to Compatriots of the Nation," May 17, 1989. Translated documents cited throughout this article were gathered in Beijing during the spring demonstrations and were provided courtesy of Mr. Robin Munro of *Asia Watch*, New York.

Fifth movement when it was claimed "the students and the masses stopped at a low level of consciousness by just aspiring for a good bureaucrat to replace the bad one," now the students and even the workers were committed to creating a "new politics" totally separate from the Communist hierarchy.[5] As a clear demonstration of their independence, student leaders thus rejected attempts by sympathetic Politburo members, such as Hu Qili, to get the students to tailor their actions to shifting internal power relations among the top leadership.[6] Playing to certain factions within the party, it was believed, only strengthened the people's "dependency" on centralized authority: "All [we] can do is to swear allegiance to whoever is in power. This dependence in turn allows those who possess a certain degree of authority to consolidate their power."[7] Writing in early March, student leader Wang Dan thus urged the Chinese people to learn from their Eastern European compatriots that "democracy is not given but must be fought for by the people from below."

Popular assault on political dependency—especially the traditional reliance on the "great leader"—was perhaps the most fundamental psychological transformation in the emergence of Chinese civil society. Although public denunciations of the leader cult have occurred in previous movements in China— often encouraged by CCP propaganda—the spring demonstrations produced the most widespread articulation of the anti-leader theme since Mao Zedong's death. The collective energy

---

[5] Chinese People's University Ph.D. candidate, "The 'April Student Movement' and 'April Fifth Movement'—A Comparative Analysis that the Authorities Tried Desperately to Avoid," May 1, 1989.

[6] According to Wu'er Kaixi, Hu's envoys warned the students that the demonstrations were shifting the power balance in favor of Politburo hardliners, but they were rebuffed out of a desire to make a clean break with "old-style" bureaucratic politics. People's Liberation Army generals also sent representatives to "make a deal" before the declaration of martial law, which the students also rejected. Interview, summer 1989.

[7] University of Science and Technology, Beijing Students' Autonomous Federation, "What Do Factional Disputes Reveal?," May 25, 1989.

produced during the demonstrations led the people to declare their supremacy over the leader as was evident in the many irreverent posters and student-led chants deriding Deng Xiaoping and especially Li Peng, who was even pictured as Adolf Hitler. One student chant was especially derisive of Deng Xiaoping: "How are you Xiaoping, how confused are you?" (*Xiaoping ni hao, ni hao hutu*). Along with elaborate posters portraying Deng as the old Qing dynasty dowager Ci Xi, this irreverence probably drove the top leadership up the wall, though it also crystallized in the popular mind a clear delineation of the people versus the state. On the other hand, the students' admiration for the deceased Hu Yaobang and, even more so, Mr. Gorbachev, indicated the continued appeal of a strong liberal leader.

For decades, it was claimed "the invincibility of Mao Zedong . . . had created in the people a psychological dependence: to defend one's position in the revolutionary line-up, and thus one's survival, one had to rely on an able or powerful leader."[8] But now the focus was on disassociating from the "patriarchal" leader, a theme that was often intertwined with declarations of independence from one's parents. "In the past I thought of myself as the Mao Zedong of China," one student is quoted as saying during the debate over the hunger strike. "It is only today [10 May] that I find that I am nobody. I love my parents, but I love my mother country more."[9] Throughout the history of the PRC, China's leaders have, I believe, strengthened their authority by "infantilizing" the population, that is, treating the entire Chinese nation (including the elderly) as though they were children. Despite its deep roots in Chinese political tradition, especially the notion of bureaucrats as "parental officials" (*fumu guan*), participants in the demonstrations

---

[8]"What Do Factional Disputes Reveal?" According to Su Shaozhi, "many old leaders are still influenced by Mao's ruling style." Interview, fall 1989.

[9]Quoted in Chai Ling, "I Was Willing to Sacrifice Myself to Allow Students to Live On." Written "before and after" the hunger strike.

finally rejected this patriarchalism—an act best symbolized by the fact that young students (and even children) took the lead in challenging the government. In addition to Wu'er Kaixi's well-known challenge of Li Peng during the televised dialogue, observers of the demonstrations noted the incredible assertiveness of young children even in face-to-face confrontations with police. This was epitomized by one placard reading "Children declare: Long live the university students!" held by what appeared to be a five-year-old. That many elderly people were so exuberant during the demonstrations reflected, perhaps, a feeling that spring 1989 constituted their last chance to escape from a lifetime of "infantilization" by the government. It was noticeable that during and after the crackdown, speeches by Yang Shangkun, Jiang Zemin, and Wang Zhen revived the condescending, "childlike" treatment of the students and the general population. By contrast, true to Rousseau's theory, Beijing's citizens were "obeying not a single person [i.e., parent or great leader], but the decision of their own wills."

The separation of society from "patriarchal" leaders and the totalitarian state was also reflected in the specific political demands and spontaneous organization established by the students, workers, and even peasants. Freedom of the press and speech were especially important. Student leader Wang Dan argued that a critical attitude from an independent standpoint had to be maintained. Otherwise, the people would simply remain adjuncts to the party and government and their fate would not improve. Similar arguments led many groups to look to the National People's Congress (NPC) to solve the current crisis and begin the transition to democracy. As the only body theoretically "representative" of the Chinese people, the NPC offered an institutional structure for bringing the people's will to bear on the law-making process. While calls were also made by disaffected party members to reform the Communist Party in line with proposals often made, ironically, by Deng Xiaoping, workers asserted their right to "have the function of supervising the CCP.''[10] Most important, the population expressed its independence by organizing a variety of ad hoc groups and "autonomous" organs, including opposition political parties. Although the government-imposed "units" (*danwei*) served as a basic foundation for organizing the mass demonstrations, new groups appeared throughout the country. Autonomous student groups were established on most campuses—including relatively isolated areas like Guizhou, Shanxi, Gansu, and Qinghai —while unions sprouted up in Beijing, Hangzhou, Inner Mongolia, Changchun (Jilin), and even Nanchang (Jiangxi), where workers modeled their union after Poland's Solidarity. As in previous political conflicts, railway workers seemed particularly active. This led to strong postcrackdown measures against them. There were also the so-called city residents' groups and self-government associations, such as in Qingdao and Kunming, and many parts of Anhui where considerable local organization and demonstrations apparently occurred. While entrepreneurs in the Northeast formed their own "federation" (evidently to protect newly acquired property rights), several political parties were organized in Beijing, Qinghai, and Dalian, where the China Democratic Political Party reportedly "sent letters of appeal to other provinces and cities." Although formation of political parties was a rare act during the popular movement, it demonstrated growing distrust of the CCP and a sense of popular political responsibility characteristic of civil society. The extent of popular organization was indirectly attested to by the government's postcrackdown regulation "on the registration of social organizations, the first such measure since 1950," which makes spontaneous organization much more difficult.

---

[10] BWAF Preparatory Committee, "Beijing Workers' Autonomous Federation Preparatory Program," May 21, 1989. Proposals for party reform included many openly discussed since 1978, such as restrictions on "special privileges" and vesting authority in institutions instead of persons. See Some Cadres of Central State Institutions, "Letter to the People," May 19, 1989.

Popular Unity and Civil Society

> Who so gives himself to all gives himself to none.
>
> —Rousseau

The emergence of civil society in China was also reflected in the major breakdown of traditional social divisions as various groups asserted the collective good over their parochial interests. Class tensions between workers and students had prevented the 1986 demonstrations from ballooning into mass actions and were still evident in the early stages of the 1989 actions. Yet, by the simple act of declaring and then carrying out a hunger strike, the students announced to the nation that, contrary to popular belief and ongoing government propaganda, they were not demonstrating merely for personal gain—better job placements and higher pay—but to save the nation from the scourge of corruption and nepotism that was destroying the economy and social fabric. Whereas the government's post-1986 propaganda denouncing purported student ''selfishness'' had apparently swayed the population, now the political tables were turned: the hunger-striking students were selflessly sacrificing their careers and even lives for patriotic goals, while the CCP leadership was protecting individual and family interests. During the revolution, the Communists had established their political legitimacy by risking their lives to penetrate factories and bring the ''truth'' about Kuomintang (Nationalist Party) corruption to the workers, but now it was the students who were defying authority by trying to mobilize workers behind the sacred national cause. Indeed, students attempted to enter factories and mobilize workers in many cities, including Beijing, Wuhan, Dalian, and Harbin, often supported by ''citizen support teams.'' ''Patriotic'' was not just a term adopted for tactical reasons, but a sentiment that expressed mass admiration for the students, especially in Beijing where protecting ''our university students'' (*women de da xuesheng*) became a popular rallying cry.

The unity among students, workers, and even some soldiers

was also evident in the various announcements and big-character posters issued by their respective groups and individuals. True to Rousseau's dictum that a people constituting themselves as an "association" will override self-interest and defend all of their members, the primary obligation of the budding worker organizations was not to press for higher wages and immediate payoffs, but to join with and protect the students. The new "president" of Beijing's "City Construction Workers' Autonomous Federation" asserted that "the students are protesting for the people" and so "we workers of China are Chinese sympathizing with the student brothers and sisters."[11] "The national crisis is ahead," he emphasized, and thus "each individual has the responsibility [so that] the working class from all sections, all professions, must unite together and protect our students." Students and workers alike were now identifying their individual, *personal will* with the national interest, putting aside the divisions that had obstructed a united front ever since the first expression of popular discontent in the late 1970s.

This linking of the individual to the nation—a central concept in Rousseau's vision of civil society—ran through most of the public statements issued by the fledgling workers' movement. An early "public notice" by the Beijing Workers' Autonomous Federation (BWAF) thus proclaimed "maintaining close cooperation with the Students' Autonomous Federation" as one of the primary functions of its hastily organized "worker picket group."[12] For other workers, the students' action was seen not only as representing the popular will, but as making previously quiescent elements of the population aware of their new-found responsibilities to the nation. "Your righteous action has stirred

---

[11] Pamphlet, "Aim of the City Construction Workers' Autonomous Federation," May 21, 1989. That the popular movement expressed a basic Chinese national identity was felt by people in Hong Kong and Taiwan as well as China, even before the crackdown.

[12] BWAF Standing Committee, "Beijing Workers' Autonomous Federation, Public Notice No. 5," May 21, 1989.

the feelings of the workers, the feelings of the whole society. You have voiced out the words from our heart. Your feelings of grief and anxiety toward the country is the same as our feelings. The rise and fall of the nation is the responsibility of each individual."[13] The students were also an inspiration for workers to begin organizing opposition to the CCP, which has traditionally maintained tight control over the workplace. Noting that the students had generated a "nationwide patriotic movement . . . which directly affects the interests of the workers," the BWAF announced in its May 19 Declaration, with the apparent intention for workers in other cities to follow suit, that "the Beijing workers have become organized." On May 21, after asserting that the "People's Republic of China is led by the working class," the BWAF claimed "every right to drive out the dictators" and to "promote democracy." So that rank-and-file workers understood that such a dramatic change could not occur without concerted action, they emphasized that "our source of power comes from unity, our source of success comes from unbreakable belief." In the spirit of the emerging civil society, worker propaganda stressed unity and national purpose over class and "trade union" interests.

The emphasis on national unity and solidarity also led the workers to warn students against pursuing a narrow agenda and political tactics that might alienate rank-and-file workers. Despite the exclusion of workers from many student-organized activities on Tiananmen Square (and the refusal of students to respond to the offer by some workers to initiate strikes before the crackdown), the workers understood—perhaps better than the student leaders—the necessity of presenting a united front to the CCP. In fact, early government warnings that possible student alliances with workers constituted a "counter-revolutionary" act inhibited initiatives toward the workers. According to one worker's "open letter" to students issued soon after the provocative April 26

---

[13] "Beijing Workers' Open Letter to Students," April 23, 1989.

People's Daily editorial, "You must fight for the wide support of all the workers, farmers, soldiers, and proprietors. But how to gain their support? First, do not [place too much] emphasis on the treatment of intellectuals and the higher education budget, and do not cry for democracy impractically. For this would affect the relationship between the students and the workers and farmers, and is harmful to unification." Overall, the students heeded this advice as their demands spoke mostly to national issues while generally avoiding parochial student interests.[14] The students also indicated their considerable indebtedness to Beijing's workers, especially the pickets. "Thank you for your hard work. For more than a month, you have given wide support to this great patriotic movement. . . . When we marched on the streets, you applauded and cheered us on, gave us food and water, even donated all your savings unselfishly. . . . Without your support, we could not have held on until now. You honorable people, usually you are common and plain. . . . [But] before you, the apparent strength [of the government] becomes comparatively small and pitiful."[15] "Workers, farmers, soldiers, students, and businessmen" should, the document concluded, "unite and fight for democracy for the People's Republic of China," while class differences should be put aside, subordinated to the collective popular will demanding democratic change.

Perhaps the greatest indication of solidarity between students and Beijing's population was the latter's paternal concern for the hunger strikers. While student motives for demonstrating were often suspect in the popular eye, the decision by hundreds of students to put their lives at risk generated enormous popular response—the single most important factor in crystallizing civil

---

[14] Students arguing in favor of vacating the Square as a way to receive "a record of merit with the government" and suggesting they could always go abroad to study were thus strongly criticized by student leader Chai Ling. See "I Was Willing to Sacrifice Myself."

[15] Beijing Teachers' College Students' Autonomous Federation, "To the Workers' Picket Group," May 28, 1989.

society. Reacting to the government's blatant disregard for the students' sacrifice (an intransigence in the face of popular remonstration that even the traditional imperial state would never resort to), workers and city people, including many medical personnel, responded with overwhelming care. Thus, on May 20, the BWAF declared that "supporting and protecting the student hunger strikers" was its primary goal, while another worker organization pledged to defend the "300,000 [sic] university students . . . on hunger strike [who now] face the threat of a strong and brutal suppression."[16] While some workers were still reluctant to join the demonstrations out of fear of persecution and loss of employment, they offered to "raise money and provide equipment" even before the beginning of the hunger strike. Even sympathetic soldiers lamented their inability to join the demonstrations but expressed their overall support. Suddenly, the student hunger strikers epitomized the entire Chinese nation and the plight of millions who had been ignored by a government that has often been more willing to see people die than respond to popular interests.[17]

The flip side of this collective will to protect student hunger strikers was a broad denunciation of government corruption. To the extent that civil society involves a conscious subordination of individual and group interests to the common good, the selflessness of the students was held up in great contrast to the self-serving actions of China's political rulers. Throughout the public statements by workers, students, and even party members ran heartfelt complaints that government corruption violated the

---

[16] "BWAF Preparatory Committee Public Notice No. 1," May 20, 1989, and Chinese Workers' Movement College Committee in Support of Student Action, Capital Workers Picket Group Temporary Command Center, "Letter to Capital Workers," no date. Such "protective" statements were quite widespread even among military leaders.

[17] Similar motives led citizens to "take care of our soldiers" who were left to languish in the sun for days by their thick-skinned leaders. "A Statement for Citizens Concerning the Army Entering the Capital," handout from Beijing University, May 20, 1989.

"public trust" and was directly responsible for the many problems in the economic reforms. Castigating the CCP's purported commitment to "serve the people," workers in particular criticized government venality, often in Marxist terms. "The propaganda to the workers, farmers, and soldiers about 'owned by the people' actually becomes 'owned by a small group of bourgeoisie,' " one very irate worker complained. "They called us 'masters of the country' and those 'masters' lived in overcrowded houses through generations. However, those 'civil servants' built their own villas. 'Masters' go to work on overcrowded buses, 'civil servants' own many luxurious sedans."[18] Some workers even wanted to know "how much Deng [Xiaoping's] son placed in his bet on horse racing in Hong Kong."[19] Despite the relatively small financial expenditures involved, such "corruptions" proved that China's leaders had ceased to function as civil servants (contrary to Zhou Enlai and Mao, who were revered by some demonstrators because of their lifelong public commitment) and should, therefore, be replaced. Workers thus joined the students in demonstrating their political sophistication by calling for an emergency meeting of the Standing Committee of the NPC to deal in part with corruption.[20]

Concern for the common good was also expressed by the general unwillingness of workers to disrupt daily life. Although this cannot be independently verified, the government purposely withdrew police and threatened to terminate vital services, including food deliveries, to stifle popular support of the movement. In contrast, striking workers promised not only to maintain

---

[18] "Letter to Students," April 28, 1989. The government's issuance of "treasury bonds" to "cover their extravagances" drew especially harsh comment. BWAF, "Letter to the People of the Entire City," April 20, 1989.

[19] BWAF, "Ten Questions," April 20, 1989. This was the first question; the second asked how much public monies Zhao Ziyang and his wife spent on their weekend golf games. Not until the fifth question were major financial issues addressed, such as China's national debt.

[20] Workers Representative of a Factory, "Open Letter to the Standing Committee of the NPC," May 24, 1989.

"public order" but also to exclude critical services, such as "gas supply, mail and vegetable deliveries, and television broadcasting," from their strike actions.[21] While the Communist leadership was willing to threaten the lives of innocent civilians—an image undoubtedly hardened by the indiscriminate killings that occurred on June 3 and 4—the popular movement exhibited the "benevolent" protection characteristic of legitimate political authority in China's Confucian tradition. In similar terms, movement leaders strongly criticized individuals who used the demonstrations to advance their personal or narrow group interests. While the BWAF warned workers against considering the union "just a welfare organization," Chai Ling berated "vainglorious" student leaders and "students who came [to Beijing] just for the trip."[22] At the height of the popular movement (and confronted with government propaganda efforts to besmirch the students' idealism by, for example, claiming that Wu'er Kaixi threw a banquet during the hunger strike), it was absolutely vital to subordinate all individual concerns to the common interest. In classic Rousseauian terms, it was even necessary to "compel a man to be free" by restraining individuals who broke with discipline and destroyed the direction of the movement. Demonstrators who defaced Mao's portrait were thus turned over to the police, while worker and student pamphlets warned against individual acts of violence and "illegal behavior like arson, robbery, or beating people up." As Wu'er Kaixi pointed out later, however, students could do little prior to June 3 to prevent some groups from advocating violence since repression of such views seemed to violate the democratic spirit of the movement. Civil society did not mean that "anything goes." Rather, it required a self-imposed discipline, which, indeed, appeared to emerge among the vast majority of demonstrators.

---

[21] "BWAF Preparatory Committee Public Notice No. 1," May 20, 1989; and "BWAF Public Notice No. 2," May 21, 1989.

[22] "BWAF Preparatory Program," May 21, 1989; and Chai Ling, "I Was Willing to Sacrifice Myself."

Reason and Civil Society

> His faculties will develop, his ideas take on wider scope, [and]
> his sentiments become ennobled.
>
> —Rousseau

The general commitment to nonviolence reflected not only a tactical decision among students' and workers' leaders but another central theme in Rousseau's view of the "civil state": the triumph of reason over impulse. Rousseau's epigram, quoted above, captures the spirit and overall thrust of the popular movement in Beijing, which abjured violence and embraced rational dialogue. Despite numerous government efforts to provoke the students and the general population beginning on April 20 when student petitioners were beaten by police, the overwhelming response of the population was to engage the government and the military in discussion and argument. In this struggle for possession of the people's political soul, participants spontaneously realized that logic was their most powerful weapon, especially against a government that, many people evidently believed, is based on lies. While one worker lamented that in a "vast country like China, there is not even a place for 'truth,' " now the people would rely on reason to reveal the truth.[23] Thus, when government propaganda compared the current demonstrations to the Cultural Revolution, big-character posters were written that delineated the fundamental differences between the two movements in considerable detail.[24] And, when the government accused the students of creating "turmoil," they responded by citing histori-

---

[23] BWAF, "Letter to Compatriots of the Nation," May 17, 1989. Statements by journalists indicating that they had lied consistently to the public strongly reinforced this notion. Chinese dissident Su Wei has argued that persistent lying is one of the major characteristics of "Chinese Communist political culture." Talk to American PEN Conference, October 4, 1989, New York.

[24] "The Ten Differences Between the Present Patriotic Movement and the Cultural Revolution," People's University, April 30 1989. Among the many differences was the fact that the Cultural Revolution was "serious turmoil," initiated by "Chairman Mao himself," and "eternally despised."

cal evidence that it was the Communist Party that had created most major disorders, such as the Great Leap Forward and the Cultural Revolution. Similar logic was employed to justify political reforms in China, as many of Deng Xiaoping's own words, particularly his relatively "liberal" August 1980 speech, were quoted to support student demands. This reliance on rational discourse, moreover, was not only reserved to the students and intellectuals, but was also used by the city's residents to try to sway the army against entering Beijing. "Li Peng goes against his own words," an "ordinary citizen" is quoted as saying in a long tape recording of a dialogue between soldiers and students. "Yesterday he was saying that the students' activities were not turmoil. Today he says they are."[25] The fact that ordinary Beijing residents were evidently persuading the army through such rational discourse may have convinced the leadership to order the crackdown and restore a political authority based on force, not reason. Yet even during the massacre, many citizens and student leaders such as Shen Tong, relied on reason over impulse in trying to prevent oncoming troops from further killing, but to no avail.

Conclusion

Rousseau's concept of civil society is a nebulous one, and he did not establish strict criteria for verifying its creation. *The Social Contract* was a prescriptive tract aimed at the French and other peoples who had not yet made their rightful claim to "citizen." Although evidence from the popular movement in Beijing indicates that a civil society emerged in urban China in the spring of 1989, only future historical developments can bear out this proposition. The sources cited here indicate that the basic ingredients of Rousseau's concept were present: the sense of society's separation from the state, the widespread unity among disparate groups, individual identification with the nation's destiny, pater-

---

[25] "A Dialogue Between a Student from the Beijing Central Arts College and a Corporal of the People's Liberation Army in the Small Hours of June 3, 1989."

nal concern for society's members at risk, and broad use of reason. Since early June, the resilient opposition of many Chinese to the postcrackdown repression further suggests that a crystallization of collective resistance to Communist political authority has taken place. Further, it is quite clear that many work units have sought to protect their members and have even aided student leaders to leave the country. Yet cases of people informing on their neighbors and even family members to the police indicate that popular unity in opposition to the despotic state in China is far from complete. "Once the Master appears upon the scene," Rousseau so aptly warned, "the sovereign vanishes, and the body politic suffers destruction."

Seven

THE CHANGING ROLE
OF THE CHINESE MEDIA

Seth Faison

IT WAS already late evening when two young editors at the *Renmin ribao* (People's daily) approached the office of Tan Wenrui, the paper's editor-in-chief. It was unusual for the men to visit their boss at a late hour, but it had been an unusual day. More than one thousand determined students from Beijing University had marched overnight on April 17, 1989, to Tiananmen Square, where they laid wreaths for former party leader Hu Yaobang, who had died of a heart attack two days earlier. It was the largest student march since late 1986, and the newsroom was abuzz with speculation that even larger protests would follow. The young journalists were now wondering: Would the *People's Daily*, official mouthpiece of the CCP, report on the day's remarkable events?

Tan, a slim, soft-spoken man in his late sixties, was talking on the telephone. He motioned the two editors to come into his office, a spacious room whose walls were covered with citations and photographs accumulated during Tan's thirty-nine-year career as a loyal soldier for the party paper. When Tan hung up the phone, one of the journalists handed him a handwritten draft of a news article about the demonstration put together by a couple of *People's Daily* reporters who witnessed the daring march. Tan read it in silence. He knew that the editors were seeking his approval to publish it, something they had never done before. Like other official newspapers, the *People's Daily* had to follow party instructions when assigning, reporting, and especially publishing stories. Any deviation from the norm could endanger the careers of reporters and editors involved. Tan remained silent. The editors got up and left, their plea silently made.

Tan sat quietly for several more minutes, then continued his nightly round of telephone calls to editors at other newspapers to see how they were playing the officially sanctioned stories of the day: a report on industry in Jiangsu Province, another on rising workers' incomes, a third on an education conference. Tan may have discussed the student demonstration with other senior editors or government officials, but he did not have to ask anyone whether publishing would be seen as a direct challenge to the party's leaders. The next day, neither the *People's Daily* nor any of the other major papers carried anything about the march.

It appeared that censorship, exercised by veteran editors like Tan, had once again prevailed. But when the newspapers arrived in mail boxes around Beijing the next morning, there was a surprise. The *Keji ribao* (Science and technology daily), a state-controlled newspaper that usually limited its coverage to nonpolitical news, had published a factual account of the scene in the Square alongside a large photograph showing students, some with clenched fists, packed around a huge banner that proclaimed "The Soul of China." No one else had dared touch the story, let alone publish a picture portraying the students sympathetically. Copies were quickly pasted up on bulletin boards at Beijing University, drawing huge crowds all day. Journalists at other papers reacted with pride and a touch of envy. "It seemed like such a natural step; I remember thinking 'We will all be doing this soon,'" a reporter from the *Zhongguo qingnian bao* (China youth news) said later.

Sure enough, the *Science and Technology Daily*'s coverage, like a tiny leak in the dike of official control, led to further journalistic risk-taking, which eventually turned into a flood of reports on the peaceful protest movement. In the following days, balanced articles on the spreading demonstrations appeared in the *Gongren ribao* (Workers' daily), the *Nongmin ribao* (Farmers daily), and *Beijing qingnian bao* (Beijing youth news). Within a few weeks, journalists joined students to march for greater press freedom, arguing that it was a cornerstone of long overdue political reform. Inside newspaper offices, reporters including those at the *People's Daily* whose initial attempt to cover the movement had been frustrated by their cautious editor—petitioned their superiors to begin reporting accurately. Finally, after a massive demonstration on May 4, with support from the liberal faction of the party, even the *People's Daily* started to report on the protests in a fair, if limited, way. Everyone followed suit, and by mid-May, the dike of censorship itself seemed to have been washed away. But hopes that press freedom had finally arrived in China turned out to be premature, and the media revolution proved temporary. Once the student movement was suppressed, the wall of control was rebuilt faster and more completely than most journalists had imagined possible. By early June, the *People's Daily* again resembled a CCP bulletin more than a newspaper.

The brief opening of the Chinese press, however, left an indelible mark on the minds of Chinese journalists, their readers, and, no doubt, the party leadership itself. Journalists had organized themselves into a professional group demanding change, openly challenging the authority of their nation's leaders. Moreover, in a nation that looked to its newspapers to define what was officially sanctioned, and not necessarily what was true, the media's open support on May 17 of students hunger-striking for democracy signaled that it was permissible for ordinary Beijing residents to take to the streets. For the next two days, over one million people demonstrated in opposition to the government, showing decisively how much the government had lost its people's support. The ensuing sequence of events was tragic.

The *Science and Technology Daily* Breaches the Dike of Party Censorship

Chinese newspapers have been under strict control since the CCP gained power in 1949. For journalists, and especially for senior editors like Tan Wenrui, a central criterion for appointment to a job has been political reliability and willingness to follow orders. When the *Science and Technology Daily* printed its groundbreaking first report on the demonstrations, the question many journalists immediately asked was why the newspaper's editor, Lin Zexin, had allowed such a report when Tan had not. Reporters at the *Science and Technology Daily* explained later that Lin had been overlooked when top editors were called to a meeting by Hu Qili, the senior Politburo member responsible for ideological affairs, where he instructed them not to report the disturbances. In fact, when Hu met with the editors on April 19, the *Science and Technology Daily* had already run its first report that morning.

Lin must have known he was risking his job to allow such coverage, even once. The following day, after the students clashed with police outside Zhongnanhai, the CCP headquarters, the *Science and Technology Daily* used only the official Xinhua News Agency account, which journalists saw as one-sided in favor of the government. His staff urged him to report more, and the conflict came to a head at the end of the week.

Late Friday night, April 21, journalists watched more than 100,000 students march out of the darkness into Tiananmen Square to position themselves for Hu Yaobang's memorial service at the adjoining Great Hall of the People the next morning. It was a remarkable, magical scene, as students proceeded in near-perfect order into the Square, singing the "Internationale" and chanting slogans for more democracy. A few days before, no one had dared dream that so many students would risk bloodshed to demonstrate; it was by far the largest independent march in the history of the People's Republic of China, and at least one *Sci-*

ence and Technology Daily reporter said she was moved to tears. The police did not clear away the students by daybreak, as many had expected they would. But neither did Premier Li Peng nor any other leader come out to acknowledge them. Even when, in a gesture rich with symbolism, three student leaders knelt on the steps of the Great Hall of the People for forty minutes, holding overhead a scrolled list of demands, no leader dared to come out. A chance to diffuse peacefully a sizable store of protest sentiment was clearly missed, and students were badly disappointed and angered.

The reporters from the *Science and Technology Daily* who stayed up all night in the Square returned to their offices Saturday afternoon, determined to produce a detailed report on the remarkable event. One reporter said later he felt a sense of mission, knowing that other papers would be forced to limit their coverage to the memorial service itself, ignoring the protest, which was clearly more significant. But editors of the paper soon let it be known that if they ran a story describing the demonstration, distribution of the newspaper would be blocked.

The reporters did not want to give in. At a meeting that lasted late into Saturday night, April 23, younger journalists at the paper were so adamant that thorough coverage continue that they persuaded a majority of the staff to threaten resignation if publication did not go ahead. Finally, Lin agreed. The newspaper was printed, and when the authorities stopped normal distribution through the mail, editors and reporters personally carried stacks of the paper to post offices around Beijing so they could be delivered, even if half a day late. Journalists were exhilarated. The CCP, it seemed, would no longer be able to control the press completely.

Chinese Press Freedom and the Case of Qin Benli

In a decade of economic and political reform, the news media had been behind other, comparable fields of intellectual endeavor. The publishing industry, for example, had gradually absorbed outside and liberalizing influences, but the press, reflecting the daily activities and aspirations of party leaders, remained under tight supervision. Newspapers were edited to please the leadership, not ordinary readers. Political divisions were rarely even hinted at, and the personal lives of high-level cadres were strictly off-limits for reporters. Street demonstrations went unreported.

By 1988, however, minor signs of change began to appear. A handful of nonofficial newspapers—set up independently but still liable to censorship by propaganda departments—were pushing the limits of what was acceptable. A growing number of reports on sensitive economic issues were published; if somewhat one-sided, they at least brought touchy subjects out into the open, a clear step forward.

Other issues, including political ones, eventually came under journalistic scrutiny as well. One blockbuster appeared in December 1988, when the progressive, nonofficial, Shanghai-based journal, the *World Economic Herald*, published an article by theoretician Su Shaozhi that sharply criticized government policy toward intellectuals. Su asserted openly that the party's biggest mistake in the past ten years was to launch political campaigns in 1983 and 1987, implicitly challenging the leaders who had presided over them. He also took the rare step of singling out two individual officials for blame, a sure-fire way of provoking a response from party superiors.

The *Herald*'s editor, a feisty, chain-smoking journalist named Qin Benli, quickly came under fire. The Shanghai authorities, who had clashed with Qin off and on ever since the paper was launched in 1980, called him in to discuss his "resignation." Qin, with thirty years of experience in debating propaganda officials, argued that Su was an old personal friend. When he offered the *Herald* an essay he had written, how could Qin refuse? The essay was based on a speech Su had delivered at a national conference in Beijing. If it was allowed there, Qin argued, shouldn't it be published for readers in Shanghai as well?

The matter was appealed to Shanghai party secretary Jiang Zemin, whose loyalty to Beijing would six months later yield a big promotion, to replace Zhao Ziyang as general secretary of the CCP. Jiang had warned Qin in 1987, when the *Herald* was criticized for printing an interview with dissident astrophysicist, Fang Lizhi, that the newspaper could continue publication on the condition that it stick to economic issues and avoid politics. Now he lectured Qin again, saying that "many comrades" thought it might be time for Qin, age 72, to retire. But his departure might be delayed, Jiang said, if Qin wrote a statement explaining why the *Herald* had run Su's article so that superiors in Beijing could consider the issue. Qin wrote the memo and was allowed to travel to the United States in February 1989, pending a decision from the capital.

In Washington, Qin accepted an interview with the Voice of America, where he said that he was still the *Herald*'s editor, but that retirement might beckon "sooner or later," a signal to Beijing that he was adequately humble but hoped to retain his position. Qin also was able to meet President George Bush, with whom he shared a four-sentence conversation on the receiving line of an official breakfast. President Bush had just announced plans to travel to China later that month, and Qin authorized a front-page story in the *Herald* on the "interview with President Bush." Qin knew it would not look good if, when Bush arrived in Beijing, the authorities had just sacked a progressive editor Bush himself had met so recently in Washington. Talk of Qin's retirement was put aside.

When Hu Yaobang died suddenly in April, Qin saw an opportunity to broach sensitive political issues, the same way students had. He authorized the *Herald*'s Beijing bureau to invite several prominent and outspoken intellectuals to a special forum to mourn Hu Yaobang and consider his legacy. For professors and writers disgruntled with the bumpy course of reform, the debate over Hu Yaobang's sudden dismissal after the last round of student demonstrations was precisely the kind of talk the government did not want to hear.

The *Herald* prepared a special edition with the most potent extracts from the forum. Wu Mingyu, a former government official, discussed how Hu once said he had two regrets in life: his failure to protect a colleague during the antirightist campaign of the 1950s, and his agreement to make a self-criticism when he was dismissed in January 1987. Others called for a clearing of Hu's name and an honest explanation about why he lost his job— in effect, calling on the government to account for its authoritarian ways.

"The main problem China has had, up to today, is a lack of democracy. A handful of people can just talk among themselves, put aside the interests of the people, and reach an unpopular decision," said Yan Jiaqi, a political scientist who was later to escape from China to lead the Paris-based democracy movement in exile. Such statements became commonplace in the weeks that followed, but to have printed them openly in a newspaper in late April was still a risk.

When Shanghai authorities got word that the *Herald* was preparing a special edition on Hu Yaobang, they telephoned Qin to make sure their censors would get a preview, as usual. Qin said yes, and on April 21 newspaper proofs were sent over accordingly. A municipal party official called Qin the following day and ordered him to delete the most sensitive parts of the edition. Summing up the government's view of the press, the official said, "It is not allowed to publish openly any opinions that differ from the official decisions of the central authorities, especially in the current circumstances when students have taken to the streets."

To the official's surprise, Qin refused. "I want Deng Xiaoping to examine these himself," Qin said of the proofs, according to the government's account of the meeting later published by Xinhua. "The earlier he looks at them, the earlier he will enjoy popular support. If he'll examine them, we will follow his decision."

Alarmed by Qin's open defiance, the official contacted Jiang Zemin, the Shanghai party chief. According to one account, Jiang exploded when Qin walked into his office in downtown Shanghai, hurling a stream of abuse at the editor that only subsided as Jiang got around to discussing the possible ways the *Herald* staff might suffer if Qin did not agree to amend the controversial edition. Eventually Qin appeared to agree and headed back to the newspaper to review the edition. Jiang later found out, however, that printing of the original edition had already begun before his meeting with Qin. In all, the government later claimed, 160,000 copies of the banned edition were printed, several hundred of which found their way to Beijing, where they were leaked to Chinese and foreign journalists. The unsuccessful attempt to stifle the *Herald* was reported around the world.

Meanwhile, the paper's staff in Shanghai took their time printing the revised edition. Qin left the city for a resort in the suburbs where he could not be reached. Other editors worked with deliberate lethargy, apologizing insincerely when Shanghai authorities called to inquire about their progress. Qin returned two days later. Instead of putting out the new edition, however, he wrote a letter to the municipal party committee saying that, "in view of the strong repercussion in the international community, it would be best to approve printing of the original edition." Qin even said he had heard that the central authorities were now considering the possibility of issuing a new official line on Hu Yaobang. This was clearly not true, at least in any formal sense. Nonetheless, it was Qin's way of warning Shanghai leaders that with an open-ended political situation in Beijing, they might be better off avoiding any rash action that could embarrass them if the liberals prevailed.

When he saw the letter, Jiang was livid. He ordered Qin dismissed immediately and sent a "work team" to the offices of the *Herald* to supervise subsequent issues. Jiang may have taken encouragement from Beijing, where Deng Xiaoping had spelled out a hard line against demonstrations that was carried in a

People's Daily editorial on April 26. According to one account, Deng personally reviewed a draft of the editorial, crossing out each use of the phrase "student movement," and replacing it with the politically charged "turmoil," effectively branding the student demonstrators as political enemies.

Only one day later, the political outlook in Beijing was muddied again, at least as far as Jiang was concerned. Student leaders, angered at being called enemies in the editorial, pulled off an extraordinary well-organized march of 100,000 fellow students, piercing police blockades with a seemingly miraculous absence of injuries. Traffic in the capital was paralyzed, and onlookers could be seen cheering the students all over the city. The government announced that some sort of dialogue with the students would be held. Deng's orders to use violence to suppress the marchers had been stymied by unwilling officials and police. The students were triumphant.

In the uncertain political climate, Jiang probably did not want to risk closing the *Herald* down entirely. He was under heavy enough criticism from the reformers as it was. But the paper's staff was not cooperating in putting out subsequent editions. For the next week's paper, the staff prepared several hard-hitting articles on a variety of topics, believing that the censors would not be able to ban everything. Arguments broke out over the final proofs. An edition was eventually prepared with a page one headline, "In Memory of May Fourth," but when it came back from the printer, a new headline had been substituted: "We Need an Atmosphere Where We Can Speak Freely." When the "work team" tried to pin down who had replaced the headline, printing staff all said they could not remember. After two more editions produced nonstop bickering, the newspaper was shut down.

At a Politburo meeting convened in early May, Zhao Ziyang castigated Jiang for handling the situation poorly. "You'll have to solve this problem yourself," Zhao reportedly said, halting discussion by other leaders who wanted to deliberate on the matter. Hearing about such support from the top, Qin Benli and the

Herald staff began rallying whomever they could. They defiantly posted hundreds of sympathetic telegrams and letters outside their office and asked influential friends in Beijing to lobby leaders on their behalf. They even began investigating the possibility of suing Jiang for "illegally" dismissing Qin, who, they argued was technically answerable to the Shanghai Academy of Social Sciences, and not to the city's party secretary. Before long, plans to take Jiang to court were being discussed openly with foreign journalists. All semblance of official control seemed to be breaking down.

Meanwhile, the Qin Benli incident became a cause célèbre in Beijing. When students again marched in huge numbers on May 4, they were joined by several hundred journalists who openly paraded under banners with the names of their newspapers and carried signs proclaiming, "Newspapers Should Speak the Truth," "Press Freedom," and "Reinstate Qin Benli." It seemed at the time that the string of uninterrupted antigovernment protests would certainly succeed in extracting some liberal concessions from the government, the first of which, many felt, would be a freer press.

The Chinese Press Opens Up

The excitement of the May 4 demonstration distracted the attention of many journalists from another, ultimately more significant, event. Zhao Ziyang, speaking to a meeting of the Asian Development Bank in Beijing, made a sharp break with Deng's hard-line stance toward the protesters. "Responsible demands from the students must be met through democratic and legal means," Zhao said in a speech that his rivals in the leadership later claimed had not been cleared through the proper channels. Experienced editors like Tan Wenrui saw immediately that Zhao, by adopting a conciliatory tone, was taking a position separate from Deng, perhaps for the first time in his long career. Zhao was apparently gambling that he could strengthen his status in the leadership, which had been declining steadily for nearly a year, by assuming a stance that obviously enjoyed more popular support than the hard-line alternative. For editors, the power struggle was now out in the open.

On the morning of May 5, it was clear which side the main newspapers were on. The *People's Daily* carried large photographs of the massive demonstration held the day before, the first time the paper had done so. In contrast to the minimal stories on the march of April 27, which had been described as illegal and improper, those published on May 5 reported accurately on the student chants for democracy and science. A photograph appearing on the front pages of many papers showed a banner that urged, "Support the *World Economic Herald.*" For ordinary readers outside Beijing, it was the clearest news yet on the demonstrations. For sophisticated readers all over China, it demonstrated the depth of the political crisis that was unfolding.

On May 5, Zhao Ziyang told Hu Qili and fellow Secretariat member Rui Xingwen that there was "no big risk in opening up a bit by reporting the demonstrations and increasing the openness of news." This statement was later used by the government as evidence that Zhao supported the protest movement; indeed, an exhibition in the Military Museum on the "quelling of the counter-revolutionary rebellion" highlighted Zhao's words, though few viewers would likely consider a call for more press freedom to be a crime. In fact, Zhao's comment simply gave official recognition to what had been a reality in the press since the previous day. An editor such as Tan Wenrui did not need to have spelled out what he had read between the lines in Zhao's May 4 speech. And Tan may have had quiet instructions from a higher authority.

Whatever the politics behind the scenes, journalists all over Beijing seemed convinced that an irrevocable step toward press freedom had been taken. "The most concrete reform to come out of the student demonstrations has been more freedom of the press. That cannot be taken away again," predicted a *World Eco-*

nomic Herald journalist—as it turned out, incorrectly. After May 5, the notion of returning to a completely one-sided media seemed impossible. But activists who were mindful of how illusory appearances can prove to be in Chinese politics began discussing how changes might be made permanent. On May 9, a group of one hundred reporters and editors marched to the All-China Journalists Association to present a petition with over one thousand signatures that demanded talks with party leaders. "The reason we are calling for such a dialogue is that our press coverage has attracted criticism at home and abroad," an editor from *China Youth News*, Li Datong, announced to applause from other journalists. "We think the press in Beijing has failed to be comprehensive and fair in its coverage. We think this is a direct result of our current press system."

Directors of the journalists' union were proud to accept the petition. Several people spoke, including a middle-aged journalist from Xinhua News Agency. "I do not approve of student demonstrations," she said. "But they occurred on the streets of Beijing in front of so many eyes. We must report these things in our newspapers." The petition requested urgent talks with party leaders over how to facilitate broader coverage of the demonstrations and ensure fairer coverage in general. It also demanded the reinstatement of Qin Benli.

Within two days, an unusually quick reaction for the CCP, Hu Qili met with a delegation of journalists at the offices of *China Youth News*. He encouraged them to speak openly, and he got what he asked for. "We are profoundly ashamed of our professional standards and ethics," said Li Datong. To illustrate the myriad controls Chinese journalists have to put up with, Li pulled out a sheaf of papers, which he said included over thirty prohibitive regulations that had been issued to journalists by the Propaganda Department over the past two years.

Others decried the past use of journalists as hatchet men in political campaigns, and one journalist sharply derided a statement made by the State Council spokesman Yuan Mu a few days earlier that all responsibility in official newspapers resided with the editor-in-chief. Every journalist in the room knew that top party leaders, especially Hu Qili himself, frequently overrode editors' decisions on the coverage of controversial issues.

Hu seemed to give a positive response. "The time has now come when journalism reform is imperative," he said, according to an account in a Hong Kong newspaper, *Ta Kung Pao*. "I know we all believe in strengthening legal procedures in journalism and speeding up journalism reform." His openness was refreshing, coming at a time when the central government was still hesitant to respond fully to month-old student requests for meetings and dialogue. Some of the journalists present must have wondered what sort of role Hu was playing in the emerging struggle within the leadership. Having worked with Deng Xiaoping since the 1950s, Hu was known as a political chameleon who was careful never to go against the senior leader. But he was closer to Zhao than anyone else in the five-person Standing Committee of the Politburo, and he would presumably want to block the ascendance of conservative rivals Li Peng and Yao Yilin. Perhaps most important, he must have been able to see that the liberal Zhao, even if he lost this battle, had the future on his side. By May 11, by one account, Zhao's conciliatory tack had gained critical support within the leadership, but its success would depend on his effectiveness in persuading the students to leave the square. Unfortunately for Zhao, the students refused to leave. And as the crisis reached its peak, Hu wavered. During Politburo meetings on the days and nights of May 16, 17, and 18—held in between and after activities with visiting Soviet leader Mikhail Gorbachev—Hu supported Zhao on one crucial vote and went against him on a second one. Although the exact procedures of those key meetings remain fuzzy, the versions that have leaked out all concluded that Hu did not fall in line against Zhao; neither did he stand with him. Hu disappeared from public view during the hunger strike and was seen again only in late September.

It is still unclear what role Hu played in the dramatic explosion of press coverage that took place on May 17, 18, and 19. For those three days, the *People's Daily* looked as though its censors had melted away. Reporters believe Hu was so caught up in the late night meetings with other leaders that he simply did not worry about media coverage. Long, detailed, and sympathetic articles on the demonstrations and hunger strikers showed no signs of the paper's earlier caution. For readers of the *People's Daily*, that was as good as official permission to go out and join the demonstrations.

At least one million people jammed Tiananmen Square and the surrounding streets on May 17, derailing parts of the Gorbachev visit. Reporters and editors from every major newspaper joined the marches, openly parading under the banners that called for a more open press. "One Million from All Walks of Life Demonstrate in Support of Hunger-Striking Students" screamed the main headline on the May 18 *People's Daily*. "Save the Students, Save the Children," read a headline over a separate story. The newspaper ran six page-one articles on the boisterous demonstration. A small corner at the bottom of page one noted the historic Gorbachev visit, which under normal circumstances would have dominated the news.

"Over one thousand reporters and workers from our own paper took part in the demonstrations, with several renowned and respected writers and editors at the head of the line," said a page-one story from one leading newspaper. Another national paper, the *Guangming Daily*, ran seven different stories on its front page about the demonstrations in Beijing and other cities. "The condition of the students and the future of the country touched the heart of every Chinese who has a conscience," said one.

As astonishing and unprecedented as such reporting was, it was not completely free. What was happening on the streets was being reported accurately and fully, but the power struggle within Zhongnanhai was left untouched. When Qian Liren, the director of the *People's Daily*, attended a meeting chaired by Li Peng on May 18, the premier is said to have exclaimed, "We have lost

control of your newspaper!'' Qian apparently responded that his
paper included ''not one small bit'' of bourgeois liberalism and
was still upholding the basic principles of the CCP.

Li Peng had more pressing matters at hand. He met student
leaders Wu'er Kaixi, Wang Dan, and others that day, and apparently did not pursue the argument with Qian. When martial law
was declared on May 20, Qian checked into a hospital, the face-
saving way of avoiding responsibility when the axe is about to
come down. Tan Wenrui also entered a hospital, as had Zhao
Ziyang the night before.

Li Peng's meeting with the unruly students was, for many
Chinese viewers, one of the high points of recent television coverage, which, like newspaper reporting, had been selective and
tame until May 17. Beijing residents had heard about Wu'er
Kaixi and Wang Dan, and the exceptional organization of student
marches on April 22 and 27 and May 4 had made them something of folk heroes. But although the two mavericks welcomed
interviewers from the foreign press, they had remained invisible
to the vast majority of Chinese. Their requests to see Li Peng
were finally granted at noon May 18 and broadcast after the
nightly 7:00 P.M. news.

Looking nervous and exhausted, Li's appearance contrasted
sharply with the smooth, if dull show he gave during a televised
meeting with Gorbachev two days prior. After hurriedly shaking
hands with the seven student representatives, commenting with
forced sympathy on the hunger striker Wu'er Kaixi's need to
wear hospital pajamas, Li launched into a rambling, disorganized
speech. He appeared confused about how to talk without a prepared agenda, especially to students whom he had until that day
referred to as unworthy renegades. ''My youngest child is older
than all of you. . . . I have three children . . . not one does official
profiteering, but they're all older than you . . . you are all like our
own children, like our own flesh and blood . . . ''

Wu'er Kaixi promptly interrupted him. ''Premier Li, we don't
have time to talk like this. . . . It was not you who invited us here,

but rather it was the huge number of us in the Square who asked you to come and talk about several issues. It should be for us to decide about what.''

Chinese viewers had never before seen one of their top leaders talked to in such a manner, much less by a twenty-one-year-old student. If television has an equalizing effect, putting debaters on a seemingly equal footing, Wu'er Kaixi's brash, charismatic manner made him look far more authoritative than Li. Other students spoke rationally, consistently and to the point. Li was mumbling incoherently even as he left. It seemed shocking that Chinese television would allow such embarrassing footage to be broadcast to hundreds of millions of viewers across the nation, but one of Li's aides personally went to China Central Television's studios that afternoon to approve an unedited version.

The reason such footage was shown, damaging or not, became clear in Li's final statement. He warned that serious consequences would follow if the students did not leave the Square immediately. But without any major concessions from the government, no amount of pleading would get the students to leave the Square. Some viewers, offended by Wu'er Kaixi's rudeness, felt he may have forfeited the students' one shot at real negotiation. But in fact a decision had already been made by the time the meeting was held. Unknown to the students, Li had the previous day agreed with other leaders—without Zhao—to declare martial law in Beijing. By meeting the students, Li apparently tried to give the impression that the government was willing to offer them one last chance. But it was already too late.

The Chinese Press Back on the Leash

After martial law was declared on May 20, it took two full weeks before the free-wheeling situation in Tiananmen Square was brought under control. At the *People's Daily*, it took one day. Qian Liren and Tan Wenrui were gone, and a "work team" made up of order obeying editors and plainclothes soldiers entered the newspaper compound, many of them dressed as doctors in ambulances to avoid being blocked at the gate. Two reporters and five print-shop workers were arrested for their complicity in putting out an unofficial edition of the newspaper that urged on the protesters. Several senior editors told friends they would resign rather than continue working at a newspaper that would now once again tow an embattled, anachronistic party line.

But few actually did. Instead, the vast majority of reporters and editors stayed on and found ways to signal their resistance to the central authorities by sneaking irreverent news items through the censor's net. The first example occurred on May 21, only one day after martial law was declared. Coverage of the demonstrators was reined in, but at the bottom of the front page, where the one or two international news items rarely attracted the censor's attention, editors ran a story on the resignation of a prime minister in Italy. No careful Chinese reader could fail to understand that it was a swipe at China's own prime minister, Li Peng. The following day, the censors had apparently not yet caught on, for in the same space was an item on a Hungarian leader's statement that Stalinist tactics of violence should not be used to suppress the people.

The new ideologues now supervising the *People's Daily* gradually tightened their grip. A box that appeared on page one to remind readers each morning how many days the as-yet unenforced martial law declaration had been in effect was eventually scrapped. Photographs of demonstrators stopped appearing in any form. By June 3, officials had effectively stifled any overt signs of sympathy for the popular expression on the streets. After June 4, there were no more overt signs to report.

On that fateful night, when soldiers were finally ordered to shoot their way into Beijing, hundreds of journalists risked their lives to see and record the tragedy for posterity. They knew by then that their own newspapers would print nothing of the truth of what they saw. Photojournalists who witnessed the killings in Muxidi, Fuxingmen, and Xidan later hid their photographs or had them confiscated by the authorities.

One woman photographer bravely held her ground beside a line of students at Xidan, watching them fall as approaching soldiers mowed them down. After a moment of shock, she began to run down a side street, only to be fired at from behind. A bullet ripped through her back, piercing her right lung before it exited above her breast. Somehow she kept running, until she fell into the arms of bystanders who carried her to a hospital. Her shirt was soaked in blood. As a medical worker cut through her clothing to inspect the wound, he found her black journalist card and told a doctor. She was immediately taken to a hidden room in the hospital basement, where she was given immediate attention ahead of a long line of other casualties. "We have to serve you first," she remembers the doctor telling her as he dressed her injury. "We have to protect the witnesses."

Chinese journalists were indeed witnesses to the Beijing uprising of 1989, witnesses who would have to remain silent, during the repression that followed, about what they had seen. But they are unlikely to forget.

One sunny afternoon in August, when an unusual breeze kept the Beijing sidewalks from becoming too hot, Tan Wenrui was seen strolling outside his home in the eastern part of the city by a friend, a young journalist, who was cycling past. Tan cordially shook hands and explained that he was still "recuperating." He looked tired. But he perked up when his friend spoke about the political situation at his own newspaper. "You are lucky you can stay at home. You don't have to watch all this," the friend told Tan, referring to the extended investigations being carried out. The veteran editor smiled and encouraged his friend to keep working, not to give up. "You are still young," Tan said. "There are many things you can do."

Appendix

CHRONOLOGY OF THE 1989 STUDENT DEMONSTRATIONS

Stefan R. Landsberger

April 15
- Former party general secretary Hu Yaobang dies.

April 16
- Following student meetings at all universities in Beijing, dozens of posters go up, praising Hu Yaobang and criticizing his opponents. Some 800 students march from the university quarters to Tiananmen.
- *Security guards at Beijing University attempt to keep students from holding joint protests.*

April 17
- Six thousand Beijing students organize march to Tiananmen to mourn Hu Yaobang.
- A similar march is organized in Shanghai.

April 18
- Students offer list of seven demands to the Standing Committee of the National People's Congress (NPC) for discussion

Actions and statements by party, government, and army officials are in italics. Compilation of this chronology would not have been possible without the help of a number of Chinese friends, who, for obvious reasons, must remain anonymous. An earlier version appeared in *China Information* 4, 1 (summer 1989): 37–56.

with Premier Li Peng. The most important are: a reassessment of Hu Yaobang; leaders and their children should make public their annual salaries and all other sources of income; freedom of the press and publication; remuneration of intellectuals and funds for education should be increased.

- More than 10,000 people rally on Tiananmen, calling for more democracy. A sit-in is started in front of the Great Hall of the People.
- At Beijing University, the first autonomous student organization is set up.

April 19

- While a crowd of 40,000 people gathers on Tiananmen to hear impassioned speeches by students calling for freedom and democracy, more than 3,000 students demonstrate in front of Zhongnanhai and clash with soldiers guarding the compound.

April 20

- In early morning, tens of thousands attempt to force their way into Zhongnanhai, demanding to see Li Peng. Fifty thousand people continue their protests on Tiananmen.
- The "Beijing Students' Autonomous Federation" (BSAF) is set up.
- Demonstrations in Shanghai and Nanjing.

April 21

- Four hundred thousand people gather on Tiananmen to take part in the memorial meeting for Hu Yaobang.

April 22

- *The official memorial service for Hu Yaobang is organized in the Great Hall of the People.*
- *About 20,000 troops of the 38th Army stationed in Baoding, Hebei Province, are transferred to Beijing; antiriot squads are mobilized; authorities crack down on the press.*

- Despite warnings to clear the square, 50,000 students gather on Tiananmen, demanding entrance to Great Hall of the People and a meeting with leaders.
- Rioting in Changsha and in Xi'an, where for twenty-four hours martial law is declared.

April 23
- Representatives of major universities in Beijing, Shanghai, Tianjin, Nanjing, and Wuhan decide to start a boycott of classes.
- Students in Beijing declare that they dissociate themselves from the rioting in Xi'an.
- *Zhao Ziyang leaves for a state visit to North Korea.*

April 24
- Beijing students start boycott of classes.
- Journalists of various party journals and magazines demand publication of fair reports of the student protests.
- *Politburo Standing Committee convenes, presided over by Li Peng. Student movement is described as a "disturbance"; the decision to set up a small group on the student demonstrations is discussed; it is said that during this meeting, Deng Xiaoping's remarks to senior personages and veteran leaders are passed, in which he calls the students "unpatriotic" and authorizes use of force against them.*

April 26
- *In a first official reaction, a* People's Daily *editorial brands the student movement as "an act of hooliganism" and calls it a "planned conspiracy," aimed at overturning the party. The editorial is based on a speech by Deng Xiaoping and the views of Deng, Chen Yun, Li Xiannian and Peng Zhen, that the nature of the student movement has changed.*
- *Beijing Party Secretary Li Ximing threatens students with harsh reprisals.*
- *Police clear and seal off Tiananmen.*

April 27

- One hundred fifty thousand students from over forty institutions of higher learning break through human barricades, formed by the police to obstruct entrance to Tiananmen, cheered on by 500,000 citizens.
- *A meeting of Politburo Standing Committee decides to set up a small group on the student demonstrations, headed by Qiao Shi and Hu Qili.*
- *The government agrees to a dialogue with the official student unions, on condition that the boycott of classes is ended.*

April 28

- Students reject government's condition.
- Boycott of classes spreads to all institutions of higher learning in Beijing.
- The BSAF is formally founded.
- *Politburo member Hu Qili is said to have told nine major Chinese newspapers to report on the "actual state of affairs."*

April 29

- *Representatives of official student unions have televised meeting with Deputy Education Minister He Dongchang and senior officials. Government refuses to recognize legal character of BSAF; BSAF Chairman Wu'er Kaixi therefore has no right to speak and leaves the meeting angry.*

April 30

- *Beijing Mayor Chen Xitong meets with representatives of official student unions.*
- *Li Ximing warns students of "unforeseeable consequences" if protests continue.*

May 1

- Leading Chinese intellectuals call on the leadership to recognize students' request for dialogue with Li Peng and for recognition of the BSAF.

- Psychology Department of Beijing Normal University conducts opinion poll among Beijing citizens, which indicates that most support the student movement.
- *Zhao Ziyang returns from North Korea.*

May 2
- In Beijing, student leaders deliver twenty-four-hour ultimatum to government to approve their conditions for talks.
- Ten thousand students march in Shanghai, demanding freedom and democracy.

May 3
- One hundred Beijing journalists hold a meeting criticizing the crackdown on the press; they support the students.
- *Government rejects students' demands for dialogue and for recognition of the BSAF.*
- *In an official meeting to mark seventieth anniversary of May Fourth Movement, Zhao Ziyang pleads for political and social stability.*
- *Police close off Tiananmen in anticipation of announced mass demonstration to commemorate May Fourth Movement.*
- *During a press conference, State Council spokesman Yuan Mu suggests Fang Lizhi and the New York-based China Alliance for Democracy play a role in the unrest.*

May 4
- Calling for an end to dictatorship, 60,000 students, 400 journalists, and many workers march in Beijing in commemoration of May Fourth Movement, supported by huge crowds of citizens; when they reach Tiananmen, the crowd has swollen to 300,000.
- Chinese press publishes pictures and reports of the demonstration.
- *In a speech to Asian Development Bank representatives in Beijing, Zhao Ziyang declares that China is politically stable, that "the just demands of the students must be met," and that*

"we should solve the problem in a democratic and legal way."
- Demonstrations take place in Shanghai, Changsha, Nanjing, Wuhan, Xi'an, Changchun, and Dalian. Student demonstrators in Harbin and Shenyang are reported locked in their campuses.

May 5
- Conciliatory tone of Zhao Ziyang's speech seems to split the BSAF.
- "College Students' Dialogue Delegation" founded to formulate demands for discussions with the authorities.

May 6
- Student delegation hands in appeals to party's Central Committee, NPC, and State Council, demanding a dialogue.

May 7
- Student leaders at Beijing University decide to continue boycott of classes for at least five more days.
- Beijing journalists demand dialogue with government.

May 8
- Journalists ask for end to censorship to enable them to report about the student movement.
- *Zhao Ziyang reconfirms the patriotic nature of the student movement.*
- *State Council and NPC agree to hold a dialogue with the students, but not with the BSAF.*

May 10
- About 10,000 students demonstrate on bicycles to publicize their demands; they demonstrate in front of New China News Agency headquarters in support of journalists' demands.
- *Politburo convenes special meeting to discuss the student movement and the forthcoming Sino-Soviet summit meeting.*
- Thousands of students protest in Taiyuan.

May 11

- Students announce that they will stage demonstrations during the visit of Mikhail Gorbachev (May 15–18). They will invite him to visit Beijing University.

May 12

- Students announce that they will start a hunger strike.
- *NPC Chairman Wan Li leaves Beijing for official visit to Canada and United States.*

May 13

- Over 200 students begin hunger strike at Tiananmen, demanding formal talks with the government, reevaluation of student movement, and retraction of April 26 *People's Daily* editorial; "Student Hunger Strikers' Delegation" is set up as their representative organization.
- Students from Beijing University and Beijing Normal University hand in a letter to the Russian Embassy, inviting Mikhail Gorbachev to their universities.
- *During meeting of the Politburo Standing Committee, Zhao Ziyang demands retraction of April 26* People's Daily *editorial; his proposal is outvoted 4 to 1.*

May 14

- Students ask Li Peng and Zhao Ziyang to go to Tiananmen for talks.
- Over 200 teachers at Beijing University hand in a letter to the government, asking it to talk with the students. In the "May 14 Manifesto," leading intellectuals such as Yan Jiaqi and Su Shaozhi express support for hunger strikers.
- Seventeen hunger strikers start to refuse fluids.
- *A dialogue between low-level leaders and students is broken off when no guarantees for a television broadcast of the talks can be obtained.*

May 15

- Gorbachev's arrival in Beijing is overshadowed by the continuing hunger strike and the presence of more than 150,000 demonstrators in front of Great Hall of the People on Tiananmen.
- Thousands of Beijing residents support the hunger strikers.
- *Chinese authorities are forced to adjust official program of Gorbachev's visit. They urge students to return to their campuses and not to harm the summit meeting, promising that no "accounts" will be settled afterward.*
- *Zhao Ziyang and Hu Qili agree with the demand of freeing the media.*

May 16

- Student protests on Tiananmen continue, with hundreds of thousands of supporters from factories, (government) offices, newspapers, and schools flocking to the Square. They are joined by representatives of some of the "democratic" parties.
- Number of hunger strikers has increased to over 3,000; 500 people have lost consciousness.
- *In a conversation with Gorbachev, Zhao Ziyang indicates that Deng Xiaoping is still the nation's "supreme leader."*
- *In a meeting of the Politburo Standing Committee attended by Deng Xiaoping, Zhao Ziyang proposes to accept a number of student demands; again he is outvoted 4 to 1.*
- In Taiyuan, some 400 students start a hunger strike.

May 17

- Over 4,000 students begin a sit-in in front of Zhongnanhai.
- Over 1,000,000 Beijing residents take to the streets supporting demands for more democracy. Organized worker participation in the demonstration almost amounts to a general strike.
- More groups and organizations write open letters to the government, appealing for a dialogue with the students.
- *Zhao Ziyang sends a message to the hunger strikers on behalf of the Central Committee and State Council, recognizing "the*

patriotic spirit of the student movement,'' and promising that no reprisals will take place against students.

- *During a meeting at his home, Deng Xiaoping proposes implementation of martial law; he is supported by a number of Standing Committee members. Zhao Ziyang expresses his disagreement.*
- *At 8:00 P.M., Zhao Ziyang tells a meeting of the Politburo Standing Committee that he cannot carry on as general secretary. The meeting approves implementation of martial law, but does not accept Zhao's resignation.*
- Over 300 begin a hunger strike in front of the mayor's office in Shanghai. Demonstrations erupt in more than twenty cities.

May 18
- Despite torrential rain, over one million Beijing citizens, students, and even soldiers turn out to demonstrate.
- By donating 100,000 *yuan* to the students, the All-China Federation of Trade Unions announces its support for the demonstrators, urging dialogue and declaring that production in many factories is affected.
- Hunger strikers take up positions in front of Zhongnanhai.
- Official media freely report developments.
- *Li Peng and other government officials meet with student leader Wu'er Kaixi and others; the meeting is broadcast on television. After an hour, talks are broken off because of Li's refusal to discuss the students' demands. Li's parting words are: "You have gone too far."*
- *A similar meeting, lasting 3½ hours, but as fruitless as that in Beijing, takes place in Shanghai.*
- *Zhao Ziyang, Li Peng, and others visit hunger strikers in hospital in an attempt to persuade them to give up their protest.*
- Tens of thousands of students demonstrate in Shanghai during last part of Gorbachev visit. In Hohhot (Inner Mongolia), more than 15,000 students demonstrate to support student hunger strike in Beijing.

May 19

- Students announce an end to hunger strike.
- *Zhao Ziyang, visiting hunger strikers at Tiananmen, tearfully acknowledges validity of students' demands and declares his support, but confesses that he has "come too late."*
- *At midnight, Li Peng tells a meeting of party, government, and military representatives that martial law in parts of Beijing has been approved and will be in force as of 10:00 A.M. the next day. Zhao Ziyang does not attend the meeting, claiming ill health.*
- Four hundred thousand demonstrators join the sit-in in front of Shanghai party headquarters. Large-scale demonstrations take place in Hangzhou, Wuhan, Xi'an, Tianjin, and other cities. A riot breaks out in Urumqi.

May 20

- *Beijing government is authorized to enforce martial law; soldiers are ordered into the city. An estimated 250,000 troops take up positions around the city and media offices. The action is said to be not directed against the students.*
- Large crowds of Beijing citizens and peasants in suburbs build road blocks to stop the army.
- Students decide to continue nonviolent protest; some resume hunger strike.
- Workers at the Shoudu Iron and Steel Works go on strike.
- *Reporting by foreign broadcasting networks is virtually stopped by martial law authorities, and satellite links are cut.*
- In Shanghai, unarmed troops try to end demonstrations.

May 21

- Over one million Beijing residents protest against martial law. Roadblocks to stop the army are built to support the students. Some military units fraternize with demonstrators.
- Students end their hunger strike.
- In open letter, the BSAF demands Deng Xiaoping's and Li Peng's resignations.

- *Troops occupy offices of the state-controlled media.*
- Demonstrations in support of Beijing protesters take place in Xi'an and Shanghai.

May 22
- Over 100,000 people, representatives of literary circles, journalists, and citizens, march in Beijing to protest martial law. All circles appeal to Wan Li to return to Beijing to convene an NPC meeting to dismiss Li Peng.
- *One hundred senior military leaders send a statement to Li Peng, refusing to deploy army units "to shoot the people." An estimated 300,000 troops have massed around Beijing.*
- *NPC Chairman Wan Li, visiting Canada and United States, criticizes measures taken by Li Peng and declares need to "firmly protect the patriotic enthusiasm of the young people in China."*
- *NPC members start gathering signatures needed to convene special NPC session to discuss legality of martial law.*
- Chinese authorities start jamming Voice of America broadcasts to deprive the demonstrators of one source of information.
- *Li Peng, Yang Shangkun, Qiao Shi, and Yao Yilin speak at a secret enlarged meeting of the Politburo to explain necessity of martial law and accuse Zhao Ziyang of supporting the student movement.*
- *Television announces that martial law-type restrictions have been imposed in Wuhan.*
- Large demonstrations take place in Shanghai, Nanjing, Kunming, Shenzhen, and other cities.

May 23
- In parts of Beijing, People's Armed Police forces clash with civilians who have erected barricades to block their advance on Tiananmen. In one incident, forty persons are reported to be severely injured.
- Hundreds of thousands of demonstrators, including officials

and staff members of party and government organizations, demand resignation of Li Peng.

- Portrait of Mao Zedong, hanging in Tiananmen, is smeared with paint. Students turn in three suspects.
- Student leader Wu'er Kaixi proposes that demonstrators leave the Square.
- Students convene a meeting and decide that their organization is not strong enough; a seven-person "Temporary Headquarters of the Student Movement," led by Chai Ling, is set up, with "Student Hunger Strikers' Delegation" functioning as the backbone.
- Beijing Independent Intellectuals Association is formed, headed by Yan Jiaqi.
- *New China News Agency reports criticism of Li Peng.*
- *Martial law regulations applying to the media are relaxed, and satellite links are restored.*
- *Wan Li, claiming health problems, cuts short his visit to United States and returns to China.*
- *Foreign Minister Qian Qichen declares that Zhao Ziyang is still party general secretary.*
- In Shanghai, tens of thousands of demonstrators demand resignation of Li Peng; 200,000 demonstrators march in Canton, demanding end to martial law and Deng's and Li's resignations.

May 24

- Rally at Tiananmen continues.
- Because his proposal to leave the Square is rejected, Beijing student leader Wu'er Kaixi is replaced.
- The name of the "Temporary Headquarters of the Student Movement" is changed to "Headquarters to Defend Tiananmen Square," headed by Chai Ling.
- *According to New China News Agency, Wan Li arrives in Shanghai, where he is met by Jiang Zemin and hospitalized.*
- *Beijing Government cuts satellite links, virtually ending*

Western television coverage of the events.
- *An enlarged meeting of the Central Military Affairs Commission is held. Yang Shangkun delivers a speech to obtain the general support of the army.*
- Demonstrators in Shanghai, Nanjing, Xi'an, Wuhan, and Changsha demand the resignation of Li Peng.

May 25
- The rally at Tiananmen demanding the resignation of Li Peng continues, although the number of demonstrators decreases. Students from other parts of China are stopped on their way to Beijing.
- "Workers' Autonomous Federation" is formed in Beijing.
- To coordinate activities of the various organizations, the "Consultative Joint Committee of All the Capital's Groups" is set up.
- *Li Peng appears on television, greeting ambassadors, and declares that Deng Xiaoping, not Zhao Ziyang, is the leader of the reforms.*

May 26
- Yan Jiaqi and Bao Zunxin publish an open letter to Li Peng, calling on him to resolve China's problems in a democratic and legal manner.
- *In party circles, documents stating the accusations against Zhao Ziyang circulate in the form of a report of the May 22 secret enlarged meeting of the Politburo.*
- *Peng Zhen meets with NPC deputy chairmen to obtain their agreement with the declaration of martial law.*
- *As the last of the military regions to do so, the Beijing military region comes out in support of martial law.*

May 27
- Student activists Wu'er Kaixi and Wang Dan announce to end the protests on Tuesday May 30 with a last big demonstration.
- *Li Xiannian acknowledges existence of a power struggle in the party.*

- *In a televised broadcast, Wan Li announces his support for martial law but describes the nature of the student movement as patriotic.*
- *In a statement carried by the media, Li Peng claims that "people in the leadership" have created confusion in China.*

May 28
- Radical students decide to remain in the Square until June 20, when the Standing Committee of the NPC is scheduled to meet; 100,000 students demonstrate for more democracy and the resignation of Li Peng and Deng Xiaoping.
- *Student leaders are warned that they can be arrested for being agents of Zhao Ziyang.*
- In Shanghai, 100,000 people protest the state of martial law in Beijing.

May 29
- Less than 10,000 students, mostly from the provinces, are left on the Square; popular support seems to be declining.
- Among some 300,000 onlookers, students erect a 27-foot plaster and styrofoam Goddess of Liberty, symbolizing their calls for democracy, in central Tiananmen.
- *Peng Zhen comes out in support of Li Peng.*

May 30
- The Goddess of Liberty is unveiled, watched by hundreds of thousands of spectators.
- After protesting about the arrest of three of its leaders, the Autonomous Workers' Federation is officially founded.
- *The government acknowledges the arrest of eleven members of the "Flying Tiger Motor Brigade," the demonstrators' liaison unit, for disturbing public order.*
- *On state television, the Goddess of Liberty is strongly criticized.*

May 31

- BSAF organizes big demonstration in support of those arrested.
- Student leader Chai Ling announces that the students want to solve problems in a peaceful way; she demands withdrawal of the army and confirmation that people who joined the movement will not be punished.
- *In an attempt to win over public opinion, the government organizes demonstrations in support of its policies in the suburbs of Beijing. Effigies of Fang Lizhi are burned, and he is accused of being a behind-the-scenes organizer of the protests.*
- *In a conversation with Li Peng and Yao Yilin, Deng Xiaoping declares that he is in favor of reform and against corruption; he states that he has asked for Li Xiannian's and Chen Yun's ideas regarding the situation, and that he has received their approval; finally, he declares that Shanghai Party Secretary Jiang Zemin will be the core of the new leadership.*
- *Wan Li arrives in Beijing.*

June 1

- *More government-organized "antiturmoil" demonstrations take place on outskirts of Beijing.*
- *Martial law restrictions in Beijing ban much foreign news coverage, prohibit interviews with Chinese citizens, and mean that all media reports in the capital must receive official approval.*
- *Army employs various methods to infiltrate demonstrators at Tiananmen.*

June 2

- Over 100,000 crowd into Tiananmen when popular singer Hou Dejian and three others start a hunger strike.
- At least three citizens are killed by a military vehicle racing out of Central Television Headquarters.
- *At least 1,000 soldiers march in the immediate vicinity of Tiananmen.*

- *In one government-organized "antiturmoil" demonstration on the outskirts of Beijing, three men dressed as Uncle Sam mock the democracy movement.*
- *All-China Federation of Trade Unions' leader Ni Zhifu attacks the Workers' Autonomous Federation.*

June 3
- Masses of Chinese students and citizens of Beijing prevent tens of thousands of unarmed troops from clearing Tiananmen.
- Tiananmen University of Democracy is formally established.
- *At 6:30 P.M., Beijing municipal government and Martial Law Headquarters issue an emergency notice, urging all Beijing residents not to go onto the streets or to the Square.*
- *At 10:00, troops receive orders to proceed to the center of Beijing and to clear the Square by 6:00 the following morning.*

June 4
- *Shortly after midnight, hundreds of tanks and armored car columns move in from the west; during their advance, pitched battles between civilians and troops are fought at the Shoudu Iron and Steel Works, Fuxingmen, Muxidi, Liubukou, Xidan, and Yongdingmen. Troops use automatic rifles, explosives, bayonets, and tanks against unarmed citizens trying to block their advance. At least 500 people are killed.*
- *After breaking through the barricades thrown up by citizens, tanks and armored cars encircle Tiananmen; using the network of underground tunnels, thousands of soldiers appear from the Great Hall of the People and crack down ruthlessly on the people left there; the encirclement of Tiananmen is completed and the Square is turned into a military encampment.*
- *From the east, columns of tanks and armored cars enter the city as late as 5:00 A.M., shooting at everything that moves.*
- *People seeking refuge in the alleys and hutongs near Tiananmen are butchered by troops and security police.*

- *Chinese Red Cross Society estimates the number of casualties to be 2,600; immediately after this announcement, the army moves into the hospitals and takes over, clearing out the dead and wounded; all medical assistance to wounded civilians is forbidden.*
- *Armed skirmishes between troops and civilians continue all day; troops open fire on innocent bystanders, citizens turn against soldiers, hanging them, sometimes dousing them with gasoline and setting them on fire.*
- *In the afternoon, state radio announces that the army has achieved a great victory in cracking down on an "extremely small group of people attempting to overthrow the Communist Party and the socialist system and to topple the People's Republic of China."*
- Before the troops enter the inner-core of Tiananmen, singer Hou Dejian and army commanders negotiate a truce under which 4,000 to 5,000 students leave the square around 5:00 A.M.; while marching toward the universities, this column is attacked by automatic rifle fire and tanks.
- In Chengdu, protests continue while news of the Beijing massacre is trickling through. After nightfall, the use of tear gas is stopped and large numbers of security forces move in; groups of demonstrators are isolated, beaten, and stabbed. Casualty estimates range from 10 to 300 people.

June 5

- *Armored cars and tanks take up positions throughout Beijing. Troops enter living areas and alleys, opening fire on anyone who defies martial law.*
- *The government congratulates troops and police for winning "the initial victory," but warns that they should be prepared for a "long and complicated struggle."*
- *Army units appear to clash with each other.*
- Strikes protesting the massacre paralyze Xi'an, Lanzhou, Shanghai, Changsha, and Wuhan; protesters fear the imposi-

tion of martial law on Nanjing and an army attack. Fighting in Chengdu between civilians and security forces continues. The police prevent ambulances from operating.

June 6
- *Armed skirmishes between troops and civilians continue.*
- Rumors about impending civil war, caused by clashes between army units, grow stronger.
- U.S. intelligence reports and satellite photos reveal that as many as 350,000 troops have surrounded Beijing.
- *Government spokesmen appear on television, emphasizing the necessity of "class struggle." According to one, 300 people have been killed, 23 of whom are said to be students, and 6,000 wounded during the crackdown. Zhang Gong, deputy commander of Beijing Martial Law Headquarters and Political Commissar of the 27th Army, states that in clearing the Square from 4:30 to 5:30 A.M. on June 4, troops did not kill one single person. Yuan Liben recounts atrocities perpetrated against the army by the population.*
- *Martial law is declared in Chengdu.*
- Fang Lizhi and his wife Li Shuxian seek refuge in the American Embassy.
- Demonstrations take place in Shenyang, Harbin, Changchun, Dalian, Lanzhou, Xi'an, Canton, Shanghai, Nanjing, Hefei, and Wuhan.
- Angry workers in Shanghai set fire to a train that has killed at least six antigovernment protesters and wounded six others, blocking a main rail line.

June 7
- *Jianguomen diplomatic compound in Beijing is fired on and surrounded by troops in effort to frighten foreign community.*
- *Army allows a select group of Chinese journalists to visit Tiananmen, which was cleaned earlier. Army units start clearing away debris at intersections of Chang'an Avenue.*

- *Supreme People's Procuratorate relays "emergency notices" to public-security agencies throughout the country, warning them not to be "hamstrung by details" in prosecuting those accused of "counter-revolutionary" crimes.*
- Demonstrations in Shenyang and Changchun continue.

June 8
- *Li Peng appears on television, praising army representatives, for their part in restoring order.*
- *State television publicizes telephone numbers for citizens to use to report "counter-revolutionary elements" to the authorities; leaders of independent student and union groups are urged to surrender to the authorities.*
- *Inhabitants of Haidian, the university area, are warned that troops have sealed off the area and are about to move in to restore order at the universities in the neighborhood.*
- *Zhu Rongji, mayor of Shanghai, appears on television, appealing for an end to the "chaos" and warning that anyone causing disturbances will be "dealt with by the police in accordance with the law."*
- Demonstrations continue in Nanjing, Harbin, Tianjin, Xi'an, Chengdu, Changsha, and Shenyang.

June 9
- *Plainclothes police and army units move into the campuses of various universities and arrest an unknown number of people; most of the students, warned by their teachers, have already left.*
- *Troops enter the Chinese Academy of Social Sciences, considered to be a reformist think tank.*
- *Deng Xiaoping, accompanied by veteran leaders, appears on television, praising military commanders for their suppression of the prodemocracy demonstrations. Deng delivers a speech that forms the basis of the official version of the suppression, in which he formulates future policy.*

- *Official broadcasts announce the first arrests in Beijing, Lanzhou, Guiyang, and Zhengzhou.*
- Fifty thousand people demonstrate in Shanghai; demonstrations continue in Canton.

June 10
- *Some tanks and armored cars withdraw from Tiananmen, which remains heavily guarded.*
- *Continouous television newscasts of persons in handcuffs, under interrogation or signing confessions; nine leaders of Workers' Autonomous Federation of Shanghai are arrested.*

June 11
- *Government issues arrest warrants for Fang Lizhi and Li Shuxian.*
- *Unedited newsreel footage shot by foreign correspondents, video footage from demonstrations, photos taken by security forces, and even video material from traffic control cameras are used by government to round up "counter-revolutionaries"; according to the Chinese media, 474 suspects have been arrested, of which 130 are in Shanghai.*

June 12
- *Government bans unofficial prodemocracy organizations and gives police the right to shoot "rioters."*
- *More than 700 people are reported arrested in Beijing, Shanghai, Hangzhou, Chengdu, Wuhan, Lanzhou, Xi'an, Canton, Changsha, and Zhengzhou.*

June 13
- *Border control is stepped up to make it impossible for "counter-revolutionaries" to leave China.*
- *State television broadcasts a list of twenty-one wanted student leaders, including Wang Dan, Wu'er Kaixi, and Chai Ling, who are in hiding.*

June 14

- People's Daily *calls for "an intensification of class struggle."*
- *State television announces arrest of two student leaders; one is said to have been turned in by his sister and brother-in-law.*
- *Beijing Communist Party Propaganda Department releases detailed account of the events of June 3–4. The account suggests that "a certain small group of people," funded by "overseas reactionary political forces," had "plotted to arrest party and state leaders and seize political power." The group attacked the army on June 3, killing nearly 100 soldiers and policemen while injuring thousands. Although exercising extraordinary restraint, troops were forced to fire after this. As a result, 100 civilians were killed and nearly 1,000 injured.*
- More than 200 people wait in line in front of American Embassy for visa applications, watched by plainclothes police.

June 15

- *In Shanghai, three workers receive death sentence for setting fire to a train on June 6.*
- People's Daily *warns the people of Hong Kong not to meddle in China's politics by supporting the democracy movement.*

June 16

- *Foreign journalists are allowed at Tiananmen. General Li Zhiyang, political commissar of the 38th Army, accompanying them, denies that people have been killed at the Square.*

June 17

- *In televised trial, Beijing court sentences eight for beating soldiers and setting fire to military vehicles, June 3–4.*

June 18

- *Beijing Radio broadcasts that regulations governing Chinese citizens traveling abroad have been tightened: all applications for exit visas already handed in are annulled, and all citizens planning a trip abroad have to apply for a new passport, en-abling the police to reevaluate the travelers.*

June 19
- *According to state media, 1,548 arrests have been made.*
- *In a televised meeting with families of soldiers killed during the army action, Li Peng declares the "counter-revolutionary rebellion as basically over," adding that "quite a lot" of protesters will still be arrested and punished "without mercy."*
- *Thousands of troops withdraw from central Beijing.*

June 20
- *A Chinese government agency invites foreign businessmen in Beijing to a meeting to hear an important announcement; instead, the participants are filmed by a Chinese television crew, apparently for use in a news program to prove the government's contention that life has returned to normal.*

June 21
- *In Shanghai, the three men convicted on June 15 are executed before a crowd of 3,000 people, despite an appeal for clemency. In Jinan, seventeen people are executed; 10,000 people are reported to have attended the execution.*
- *Supreme People's Procuratorate declares that all appeals for clemency will be turned down.*

June 22
- *Television announces arrest of fourteen Chinese as Taiwan spies.*
- *The official number of arrests has reached 1,600.*
- *In Beijing, the seven men sentenced to death on June 17 are executed after the court turns down their appeals.*
- *Ji Pengfei, director of State Council's Hong Kong and Macao Affairs Office, declares that the "one country, two systems policy" will not change and that the joint declaration will be*

observed; simultaneously, he warns Hong Kong and Macao "compatriots" not to meddle in Chinese affairs.

June 23

- *Middle schools start a week of intensive "education in patriotism," focused on June 9 speech by Deng Xiaoping, to explain the "true nature" of the student demonstrations.*
- *The director and the editor of* People's Daily, *Qian Liren and Tan Wenrui, are replaced "for health reasons" by Gao Di, a Central Committee member associated with Li Peng, and Shao Huaze, a military man associated with Yang Shangkun and former editor of the* People's Liberation Daily.
- People's Daily *accuses the protesters of having tried to turn China into a "puppet of international capitalism" and calls for "vigilance" and intensification of class struggle.*
- *An all-points police bulletin is posted for seven prominent intellectuals, accused of agitation during the recent movements. On the list are political scientist Yan Jiaqi and his wife Gao Gao; Wan Runnan, head of the Stone Corp.; Chen Yizi, head of the Institute for Restructuring the Economy; Bao Zunxin, a prominent historian; Su Xiaokang, writer and coproducer of "River Elegy"; Wang Juntao, editor of the* Economics Weekly; *and Chen Ziming, economist at a Beijing research institute.*
- *Police raid six Beijing university campuses, arresting seventeen teachers and students.*
- *Arrests and executions are reported from Dalian and Changsha.*
- Hong Kong student activists assert that Yan Jiaqi and Gao Gao escaped from China and arrived in the colony on June 20; more dissidents and student leaders are expected shortly.

June 24

- *In a special meeting of the Central Committee, Zhao Ziyang is removed from all his posts and replaced as general secretary by Jiang Zemin, former party secretary of Shanghai; although*

*Zhao is accused of "grave mistakes and errors" and splitting
the party, and held responsible for the unrest, he is not ex-
pelled from the party. The composition of the new Standing
Committee is Li Peng, Qiao Shi, Yao Yilin, Jiang Zemin, Song
Ping, and Li Ruihuan.*

- *Central Committee communiqué calls for a continuation of
economic reforms and the "open door" policy.*
- *During police raids in Beijing, scores of students and intellectuals are arrested for their alleged role in the prodemocracy movement. One, Liu Xiaobo, a Beijing Normal University professor who had just returned from the United States, is
accused of waging "anti-Communist propaganda" and of
fostering ties with the China Spring movement in the United
States.*
- People's Daily *publishes ten Deng Xiaoping quotations.*

June 25
- *The party calls for widespread purges and prosecution of officials who supported the prodemocracy demonstrations.*

June 26
- *Central Discipline Inspection Commission, headed by Qiao
Shi, announces in a communiqué that legal prosecution will be
started against followers of Zhao Ziyang.*

June 28
- *China summons home all ambassadors for consultations during meeting scheduled on July 7; only Han Xu, ambassador to
United States, does not return.*
- *Foreign Ministry spokeswoman Li Jinhua states that Chinese
government deeply regrets EEC decision to take sanctions
against China.*
- Wu'er Kaixi and his girlfriend Liu Yan are reported to have
passed through Hong Kong after their escape from China and
are said to be on their way to Europe.

June 29
- *NPC Standing Committee convenes special session. Some members demand investigation of Hu Jiwei, who solicited NPC members' signatures to convene NPC meeting ahead of schedule to rescind martial law and dismiss Li Peng.*
- *In his first published speech as general secretary, Jiang Zemin takes a hard line toward leaders of the demonstrations but hints that most students and intellectuals will be spared in the purge and crackdown on the democracy movement.*
- *In leaked transcripts of a June 16 speech, Deng Xiaoping hints there will be limits to the crackdown and executions for "counter-revolutionary" activities.*

June 30
- *In a new assessment of the casualties on June 4, Chen Xitong reports to NPC Standing Committee that 200 civilians were killed, including 36 students, and more than 3,000 citizens were wounded; according to Chen, the damage caused by the "rebellion" in Beijing amounts to 1.3 billion yuan.*
- *One hundred twenty-six of the 132 members of the NPC Standing Committee vote in favor of Deng Xiaoping's proposal to remove Zhao Ziyang from his post as vice-chairman of Military Affairs Commission.*

July 1
- *In meeting with Daniel K. Wong, the Chinese-American former mayor of Cerritos, California, Li Peng defends the use of armed force against the student demonstrators; the lack of tear gas, rubber bullets, and other riot control gear compelled soldiers to use force. He states that during the crackdown, thirty-six students, "criminals" in his words, were killed, but they were not from Beijing universities.*
- More than 20,000 soldiers and citizens from Beijing gather on Tiananmen to celebrate sixty-eighth anniversary of the founding of the CCP.

Sources

Western Publications

Beijing Review, China Aktuell, China Review (Bert Okuley, Dick Wilson), *De Tijd* (Frénk van der Linden), *De Volkskrant* (Caroline Straathof), *Far Eastern Economic Review* (Robert Delfs, Tai Ming Cheung), *Het Parool, International Herald Tribune* (Richard Bernstein, Ed Gargan, Jim Hoagland, Nicholas Kristof, Jay Mathews, Harrison Salisbury, Dan Southerland, Michael Weisskopf, Sheryl WuDunn), *Le Monde, Libération, NRC-Handelsblad* (Willem van Kemenade, Vincent Mentzel, Hans Maarten van den Brink, Lolke van der Heide), *Newsweek* (Carroll Bogert, Melinda Liu, Rod Nordland), *Open Forum, The Economist, The Guardian* (Jasper Becker, John Gittings), *The Independent* (Michael Fathers, Andrew Higgins), *The Observer* (Jonathan Mirsky), *Time Magazine* (David Aikman, Sandra Burton, Jaime FlorCruz, Ted Gup, Richard Hornik, William Stewart).

PRC and Hong Kong Publications

Jiefang, Jiushi niandai, Renmin ribao (Overseas Edition), *Shijie jingji daobao, Zhengming.*

Radio

Gert van Brakel, Frénk van der Linden, Bob Mantiri, Peter Sackman, Caroline Straathof (Dutch radio); Mark Brayne, Simon Long, James Miles, Tony Saich (BBC World Service).

Television

Kate Adie (BBC), Brian Barron (BBC), Mike Chinoy (CNN), Oscar van der Kroon (NOS), Bernard Shaw (CNN), Caroline Straathof (NOS).

BIBLIOGRAPHICAL NOTE

Tony Saich and Nancy Hearst

COPIES or originals of the Chinese documentation referred to in the chapters are available in the *Tiananmen Archive* held at the International Institute of Social History, Amsterdam. The collection has been developed in cooperation with the Sinologisch Instituut, Leiden. An excellent chronology that also contains copies of much key documentation is Wu Mouren et al., eds., *Bajiu Zhongguo minyun jishi* (Chronology of the 1989 Chinese People's Movement) (n.p., 1989). An English-language chronology is provided in the *Ming Pao* translation *June Four: A Chronicle of the Chinese Democratic Uprising* (Fayetteville: University of Arkansas Press, 1989). An extremely valuable documentary source is *Zhongguo minyun yuan ziliao jingxuan* (Selected original documents from the Chinese People's Movement), vols. 1 and 2 (Hong Kong: October Review, 1989). A good pictorial account can be found in *Beijing xueyun* (The Beijing students' movement) (Hong Kong: Xingdao Press, 1989).

Gradually, non–Chinese-language collections of documents are beginning to appear. The most complete to date are Han Minzhu, ed., *Cries for Democracy: Writings and Speeches from the 1989 Chinese Democracy Movement* (Princeton: Princeton University Press, 1990), and James Tong, ed., *Death at the Gate of Heavenly Peace: The Democracy Movement in Beijing, April–June 1989*, parts 1 and 2, in *Chinese Law and Government* 23, 1/2 (Spring/Summer 1990). In German, there is Ruth Cremerius,

Doris Fischer, and Peter Schier, eds., *Studentenprotest und Repression in China April–Juni 1989. Analyse, Chronologie, Dokumente* (Student protests and repression in China, April–June 1989. Analysis, chronology, and documents) (Hamburg: Mitteilungen des Instituts für Asienkunde, 1990). Forthcoming in the near future are Michel Oksenberg, Lawrence R. Sullivan, and Marc Lambert, eds., *Beijing Spring 1989: Confrontation and Conflict, The Basic Documents* (Armonk, NY: M. E. Sharpe, 1990), and Suzanne Ogden et al., *China's Search for Democracy: The Student and Mass Movement of 1989* (Armonk, NY: M. E. Sharpe, forthcoming).

On the rift between the Popperian student leaders and the hunger strikers, the crucial account is Christophe Nick, "The Chinese Cohn-Bendits," in *HP Magazine*, The Hague (November 4, 1989): 57–67; translated into Dutch from French, simultaneously published in the French monthly *Actuel* and a number of other European popular magazines. Other important interviews include Michel Bonnin and Jean-Philippe Béja, "Interview with Wu'er Kaixi in Paris," in *Zhengming*, Hong Kong (September 1989): 26–28; Michel Korzec, "Chinese Schaduwen in Parijs: een gesprek met Yan Jiaqi" (Chinese shadows in Paris: An interview with Yan Jiaqi), in *NRC Handelsblad*, Rotterdam, September 9, 1989; Ming Lei, Michel Bonnin, and Jean-Philippe Béja, "Interview with Qiu Wu," in *Zhengming* (October 1989): 79–82; and the interviews with Chen Jun in *Jiefang yuebao,* Hong Kong (September 1989): 38; with Yan Jiaqi in *Zhongguo shibao*, Taipei (July 13, 1989); and with Chen Yizi in *Ouzhou ribao*, Paris (September 8, 9, and 12, 1989).

Extensive official Beijing accounts of the events can be found in "Mayor Chen Xitong's Report on Putting Down Antigovernment Riot," *Xinwen gongbao* (Information bulletin), June 30, 1989; Shi Wei, "What Has Happened in Beijing," *Xinwen gongbao* (June 1989); and Secretariat of the Beijing Municipal Committee of the CCP, ed., *1989 Beijing zhizhi dongluan pingxi fan geming baoluan jishi* (Chronology of 1989 prevention of turmoil and the putting down of the counter-revolutionary rebellion in Beijing) (Beijing: Beijing ribao chubanshe, 1989). A chronology for internal circulation is Department of Political Thought, State Education Commission, ed., *Jingxin dongpo de 56 tian* (A soul-stirring 56 days) (Beijing: Dadi chubanshe, 1989). This chronology also contains interesting information on events in the provinces. Although published only for internal reference, it was withdrawn quickly after publication.

The best of the Western quickie "I was there" accounts are Time Magazine, *Massacre in Beijing: China's Struggle for Democracy* (New York: Warner Books, 1989); and Michael Fathers and Andrew Higgins, *Tiananmen: The Rape of Peking* (London: Doubleday with the Independent, 1989). Also of interest is Scott Simmie and Bob Nixon, *Tiananmen Square: An Eyewitness Account of the Chinese People's Passionate Quest for Democracy* (Seattle: University of Washington Press, 1989). A mix of eyewitness accounts and preliminary analyses can be found in Vincent Mentzel, Tony Saich, Frénk van der Linden, et al., *Hemelse Vrede: De Lente van Peking* (Heavenly peace: The spring of Peking) (Amsterdam: Balans, 1989). Frank Niming has published an extensive account of the rise of the movement set against the background of the reform program, *Op het scherp van de snede: Achtergronden en Ontwikkeling van de Volksbeweging in China. Beijing—voorjaar 1989* (On the knife's edge: Background and development of the Chinese People's Movement. Beijing—spring 1989) (Kampen: Kok-Agora, 1990).

Initial analyses of the implications of the movement and its suppression can be found in Corinna-Barbara Francis, "The Progress of Protest in China: The Student Movement of the Spring, 1989," *Asian Survey* 29, 9: 898–915; Flemming Christiansen, "The 1989 Student Demonstrations and the Limits of the Chinese Political Bargaining Machine: An Essay," *China Information* 4, 1: 17–28; Lowell Dittmer, "The Tiananmen Massacre," *Problems of Communism* (September–October 1989); Jürgen Domes, "Die Krise in der Volksrepublik China. Ursachen, Bedeutung und Folgerungen" (The crisis in the People's Republic of China:

Causes, importance and consequences), *Europa Archiv* 44 (August 1989): 465–76; Tony Saich, "Death of a Peaceful Revolution," *Government and Opposition* 25, 1: 34–47; and Tony Saich, "The Future of China," *The Pacific Review* 2, 4: 351–57.

On the petition movement see W. L. Chong, "Present Worries of Chinese Democrats: Notes on Fang Lizhi, Liu Binyan, and the Film 'River Elegy,' " *China Information* 3, 4 (1989): 1–20. On the relationship between the petition movement and the student movement, see W. L. Chong, "Fang Lizhi, Li Shuxian, and the 1989 Student Demonstrations: The Supposed Connection," *China Information* 4, 1 (1989): 1–16. On the FDC, see W. L. Chong, "The Chicago Congress: Recent Activities of the 'Front for a Democratic China,' " *China Information* 4, 2 (1989): 127.

An article looking at the movement in terms of the broader issue of democracy in China is Andrew J. Nathan, "Chinese Democracy in 1989: Continuity and Change," *Problems of Communism* (September–October 1989): 16–29, and he follows up his analysis with his book *China's Crisis* (New York: Columbia University Press, 1990). Andrew G. Walder provides an interesting perspective to the background of the movement in "The Political Sociology of the Beijing Upheaval of 1989," *Problems of Communism* (September–October 1989): 30–40. The problem of incomplete reform and its consequences is handled in Yasheng Huang, "The Origins of China's Pro-Democracy Movement and the Government's Response: A Tale of Two Reforms," *Fletcher Forum of World Affairs* (Winter 1990). Stanley Rosen provides interesting information on student attitudes based on his research in "Political Education and Student Response: Some Background Factors Behind the 1989 Beijing Demonstrations," *Issues and Studies* 25, 10 (1989). An insight into what Beijing residents thought of the events can be found in "Beijing Public Opinion Poll on the Student Demonstrations, held on 1–2 and 7 May 1989," *China Information* 4, 1 (Summer 1989).

Information on events in the provinces is more difficult to find, but the January and July 1990 issues of the *Australian Jour-*

nal of Chinese Affairs are an indispensable starting point. The articles in these two issues will be published separately in book form, edited by Jonathan Unger, under the title *The Democracy Movement in China: The View from the Provinces* (Armonk, NY: M. E. Sharpe, forthcoming). This book covers, among others, the events in Fujian (Mary Erbaugh and Richard Kraus), Hangzhou (Keith Forster), Tianjin (Josephine Fox), and Beijing (Tony Saich).

The question of human rights in China is addressed in Amnesty International, *People's Republic of China: Preliminary Findings of Killings of Unarmed Civilians, Arbitrary Arrests, and Summary Executions since June 3, 1989* (New York: Amnesty International, 1989); Amnesty International, *China. The Massacre of June 1989 and Its Aftermath* (London: Amnesty International, 1990); Asia Watch, *Punishment Season: Human Rights in China after Martial Law* (New York: Asia Watch, 1990); International League for Human Rights, *Massacre in Beijing: The Events of 3–4 June and Their Aftermath* (New York: International League for Human Rights, 1989); and Ann Kent, *Human Rights in the PRC* (Canberra: Legislative Research Service, 1989–1990).

The international reaction to events is handled by James Seymour in "Human Rights and the World Response to the 1989 Crackdown in China," *China Information* 4, 4 (Spring 1990): 1–14; and in more detail in his forthcoming book, *The International Reaction to the 1989 Crackdown in China* (New York: East Asian Institute). See also Gary Klintworth, ed., *China's Crisis: The International Implications*, Papers on Strategy and Defence, no. 57 (Canberra, 1989).

Three of the intellectuals criticized by the regime have published works on the movement and its background: Liu Binyan, *"Tell the World": What Happened in China and Why* (New York: Pantheon, 1989); Su Shaozhi, *Understanding Democratic Reform in China*, Papers on Democracy (Bradley Institute for Democracy and Public Values, 1990); and Yan Jiaqi, *Zou xiang minzhu zhengzhi: Yan Jiaqi Zhongguo zhengzhi lunwenji* (Toward a democratic politics: Essays on Chinese politics by Yan Jiaqi) (Teaneck, NJ: Global Publishing Co., 1990). One book that promises to be fascinating reading is *Almost a Revolution* (Boston: Houghton Mifflin, 1990), written by Shen Tong, one of the student leaders.

Among the books scheduled for publication are Richard Baum, ed., *Structural Reform and Political Development in Post-Mao China* (New York: Routledge); Marta Dassù and Tony Saich, eds., *The State of China's Reforms: Problems and Prospects* (London: Kegan Paul, 1990); J. L. Hicks, ed., *The Broken Mirror: China after Tiananmen* (New York: Oxford University Press, 1990); Human Rights in China, *Children of the Dragon: The Story of Tiananmen Square* (New York: Macmillan, 1990); Peter and Marjorie Li, eds., *Politics and Conflict in China: Confrontation at Tiananmen Square, Essays and Documents* (New Brunswick, NJ: Transaction Books, 1990); and Winston Yang, ed., *Tiananmen and Its Impact* (Baltimore: University of Maryland School of Law, 1990).

Information on the role of the work unit and the system of political and social control there can be found in Gail Henderson and Myron S. Cohen, *The Chinese Hospital: A Socialist Work Unit* (New Haven: Yale University Press, 1984); Andrew G. Walder, *Communist Neo-Traditionalism: Work and Authority in Chinese Industry* (Berkeley: University of California Press, 1986); and Martin King Whyte and William Parish, *Urban Life in Contemporary China* (Chicago: University of Chicago Press, 1984). The police system is outlined in Oskar Weggel, "Der Chinesische Geheimdienst" (The Chinese secret service), *China aktuell* (June 1989): 428–32.

For a general background on pre–May Fourth Movement protests involving students see Lin Yutang, *A History of the Press and Public Opinion in China* (1936; reprinted New York: Greenwood, 1968). The most comprehensive English treatment of the May Fourth Movement remains Chow Tse-tung, *The May Fourth Movement* (Cambridge: Harvard University Press, 1963). Also of interest are Arif Dirlik, "Ideology and Organization in the May Fourth Movement," *Republican China* 12, 1 (1986): 3–19; Vera Schwartz, *The Chinese Enlightenment* (Berkeley: University of California Press, 1986); and Peng Ming, *Wusi yundong shi* (A history of the May Fourth Movement) (Beijing: Renmin chubanshe, 1984).

The May Thirtieth Movement is treated well in Nicholas Clifford, *Shanghai, 1925: In Defense of Foreign Privilege* (Ann Arbor: University of Michigan Press, 1980); Li Jianmin, *Wusa canan houde fanYing yundong* (The anti-British movement after the May Thirtieth Incident) (Taipei: Academia Sinica, 1986); and Ka-che Yip, *Religion, Nationalism and Chinese Students: The Anti-Christian Movement of 1922–1927* (Bellingham: Western Washington University Press, 1980).

The most important study of student activism of the Nanjing decade is John Israel, *Student Nationalism in China, 1927–1937* (Stanford: Stanford University Press, 1966). For the student movement in the late 1940s see Jessie Lutz, "The Chinese Student Movement of 1945–1949," *Journal of Asian Studies* 31, 1 (1971): 89–110.

For a review of student activism throughout the Republican era see John Israel, "Reflections on the Modern Chinese Student Movement," in *Students in Revolt*, ed. Seymour Lipset and Philip Altbach (New York: Houghton Mifflin, 1969), pp. 310–33. For student movements in Shanghai see Jeffrey Wasserstrom and Liu Xinyong, "Student Protest and Student Life: Shanghai 1919–1949," *Social History* 14, 1 (1989): 1–30; and Jeffrey Wasserstrom, "Taking It to the Streets: Shanghai Students and Political Protest, 1919–1949" (Ph.D. diss., University of California, 1989).

INDEX